Compiled by:

Marnie L. Pehrson

Copyright 2011, Marnie L. Pehrson

www.TrustYourHeartSeries.com
www.IdeaMarketers.com

Cover design by Sheri Brady of
MightyPhoenixDesignStudio.com

Cover Marble Backround Image
by Daniel Budiman of Dreamstime.com

All Rights reserved. The contents of this book may not be reproduced in any part or by any means without the written permission of the author.

Published by IdeaMarketers.com,
a division of CES Business Consultants

Printed in the United States of America

Library of Congress: 2011905323

ISBN: 978-0-9825878-2-9

TABLE OF CONTENTS

Acknowledgements	iii
Introduction	v
Trust the Journey - Marnie Pehrson	1
Take Responsibility for Your Life - Adela Rubio	13
A Lover's Leap - Denise Wakeman	27
The Winding Path - Stephanie Chandler	39
Shoestring Marketing - Jessica Swanson	51
Trusting Intuition When the Journey Changes - Kathleen Gage	61
Human Doing or Human Being? - Dr. Linda Miles	73
Reinventing Yourself - Milana Leshinsky	89
From ER to Entrepreneur - Ellen Britt	101
Trusting Feminine Energy in Business - Laura Howard West	115
Broadway, Broadcasting, and Business - Shannon Cherry	127
The Life Journey of a Serial Entrepreneur - Janis Pettit	141
Sometimes Things Get Worse Before They Get Better - Michele Pariza Wacek	151
What If There Was No Box? - Brian Rooney	163
Confessions of a Best-Selling Author - Leslie Householder	171
Finding Your Passion - Joanne Musa	183
Stepping Into the Unknown - Phillip Davis	195
It's All About Relationships - Lisa Rae Preston	207
How I Turned $194 Into Millions by Following My Heart - Adam Urbanski	221
Conclusion: *Miracles Await!* - Marnie Pehrson	235

ACKNOWLEDGEMENTS

A special thanks goes to Phillip Davis, my friend and "branding guy," for helping me brainstorm the idea for this book. Over the years, Phil has encouraged me to follow my heart and stay in integrity with my mission and brand of "highlighting truth and talent." I honestly wouldn't be where I am today without Phil.

I'd like to express my appreciation to all the participants in this book. I no more had the concept out of my mouth before each of them hopped on board instantly. They caught the vision of it from the outset; and I'm honored to be able to rub shoulders with such talented, experienced and wise colleagues. Each generously seeks to inspire and assist others in transforming their ideas to income.

A book of this magnitude could never be created without a good editor who has a fine eye for detail yet maintains the vision of the project. I'd like to acknowledge and express my heart-felt appreciation to my dear friend Lisa Rae Preston for her many hours of effort in editing this book. If you find any errors, they were probably due to last minute changes on my part.

Knowing that a book is usually judged by its cover, I selected Sheri Brady for the conceptualization and design of this project. Sheri captured the essence of what I intended for the book and created from scratch a compelling book cover design. It's wonderful knowing you have a book designer you can count on.

Last but certainly not least, I'd like to thank my good friend and right-hand operations manager, Luanna Rodham, for coordinating the many interviews and scheduling details necessary to promote this project effectively. For many years, I've been able to count on Luanna to handle the details in so many aspects of my business. Her consistency and reliability makes my business (and life) run smoothly.

INTRODUCTION

In compiling this book, I've gathered eighteen of my business associates from various walks of life, backgrounds and belief systems to talk about trusting your heart as it applies to business — specifically in transforming an idea to income.

I've noticed over the years that most entrepreneurs claim to follow their "gut instincts" to reap success. You'll notice each of these experts uses different terminology for this phenomenon of knowing what to do and when. They may call it following their gut, their heart, inspiration, their instincts, the Spirit, or heavenly guidance.

Some people refer to the Universe, others to God, and others their Higher Power. While I would personally call the source of my inspiration God or the Spirit, my colleagues might use different terms.

I've intentionally left in these references, allowing contributors to express in their own words what's comfortable and meaningful to them. Thus, it is up to the mature reader to glean from each example the principles and nuggets of wisdom within each expert's experience, and find the valuable truths. You are therefore invited to translate the ideas presented into terms with which you are most comfortable.

I have long adhered to the maxim, "Truth is truth where 'ere we find it." Those who are willing to lay aside differences in backgrounds, beliefs and terminology are those who find treasured truths and wisdom wherever they go.

I hope you enjoy as much as I have these stories of real people who transformed their ideas to income.

Marnie Pehrson

TRUST THE JOURNEY
Marnie L. Pehrson

In December of 1989, I gave birth to our second child, a son we named Caleb. Four hours after his birth, the nurses awakened me to say he had experienced a trauma in the nursery and was now in the neonatal ICU. His heart and breathing had stopped, and in an effort to resuscitate him, they forced tubes down his throat. The trauma of this caused seizures, so they pumped his little body full of valium. He didn't wake up to go home for 11 days.

Doctors diagnosed Caleb with SIDS and sent him home with a heart and apnea monitor. Three months later, my husband lost his job and his insurance. We were left to figure out how to pay the $600/month rental fee on Caleb's apnea monitor along with his recurring medical bills. This started a downward financial spiral from which we wouldn't fully recover for years.

My husband went into job hunt mode but didn't have any luck for several months. Finally, he suggested that I look for employment, since I had taken all the classes toward a computer degree. The only thing that stood between me and a diploma was 16 credit hours of general ed. So I started looking in the paper for jobs — many of which called for skills in Lotus 1-2-3, WordPerfect and PageMaker. I knew these software packages well. So I started applying for jobs.

One afternoon I went to an interview and came home to my baby boy and 2-year-old daughter. I remember sitting at the small kitchen table in our 1,100 square-foot home and knowing — just knowing — that if I went out into the workforce, I would never come home again. If I got a job, I would lose precious years with my children. This certainly wouldn't be true for everyone, but I knew it was for me. In hindsight, I can see even more clearly how spot-on that feeling was.

On the heels of that impression emerged an idea that would change my life. It wasn't a brand new concept, but one I'd rolled around in my head about a year earlier. In the moment I needed that idea, it returned. *Teach people computers the way other people teach piano lessons — let them come to the house and tutor them.*

The newspaper was open to the "help wanted" section, and there was a number I could call to place an ad. I didn't wait. I called it and ran this ad:

"Are you being turned down for jobs because you don't know WordPerfect, Pagemaker and Lotus 1-2-3? If so, call ###-#### for personalized hands-on training."

The $5/week ad ran in Sunday's paper, and I immediately had two students. I didn't even have any course material, so I booked the classes two weeks out and got to work. That was May of 1990, and by November of that year, I was teaching 50 hours per week with up to three people in the classes I held in a spare bedroom of our house. My students got jobs and told their employers about me. Soon I was training on-site at businesses and doing consulting and database programming.

Trust Your Heart: Transform Your Ideas Into Income

In 1994, I took what I'd learned about operating and marketing a computer training business and wrote *How to Run a Successful Computer Training Business from Home*. I had the books printed as needed - spiral bound with an acetate cover and a diskette taped in the back containing flyers, brochures, and course outlines that I used in my business. I sold the book by going on AOL, Compuserve and independent bulletin boards and uploading excerpts of the material. I included the table of contents and a sample chapter or two with my address in the back. People began mailing me checks for $24.95, plus shipping and handling.

One of the people who purchased the book was Alanna Webb of Oklahoma. Alanna struck up a conversation with me, and soon we became friends and were emailing and chatting on the phone regularly. In 1996, when Alanna suggested we create "web pages," I thought it was something she made up since her last name was Webb. I'd never heard of the Web before. She explained this new medium to me, and we went to work.

We created the first online mall in 1996. Alanna, a desktop publisher, did the web design. I did the marketing -- primarily to the local businesses with whom I was already working. We launched our mall with a free live event we held at a local university. We explained to attendees why having a web site was important and got our first batch of clients.

One of the main ways we promoted our clients was with article marketing. I produced a regular marketing tips newsletter called the "Noteworthy Ezine" and began sending articles out to other ezine editors. Also, as an ezine editor, I received article submissions from others. Whenever an article was accepted, it was customary to give credit to the author with a byline, bio and a link to their web site. This way the author could get more traffic to his or her web site.

It wasn't long before we landed a big contract for a major web design project. Alanna went full-time with the company, eventually moving to New Jersey for a while. We dissolved our partnership but stayed in touch. When Alanna returned to Oklahoma almost two years later, she'd learned a programming language called ColdFusion. ColdFusion allowed the web site visitor to load content into a web site through a web form. This was a new concept on the Web back in 1998. You see it all over the place now with content directories and social media sites like Facebook and Ning.

Alanna created her own popular site using this programming language. Shortly afterward, I had the idea to create a site that allowed writers to submit their articles to a database so that publishers could search and find articles they wanted to run. It really started as an idea for managing all the articles that were being submitted to me regularly as an ezine editor.

I ran the idea by Alanna, and she gave me her web site code and taught me the basics of ColdFusion. I tweaked what she gave me, and IdeaMarketers was born in December 1998. Along the way, the site has gone through major renovations and additions. Each of these additions started with an idea that I implemented swiftly. Not every idea I've had has worked, but the "winners" I've developed into multiple revenue streams.

One idea that stands out is the bidding system on my IdeaMarketers.com web site. The concept struck me at three in the morning. I woke up with it coming seemingly from nowhere. The next morning, I got up and programmed it and was able to start taking bids within 24 hours. The idea evolved some over the next few weeks as I tweaked the system. Now this "set your own pricing" model for advertising on the IdeaMarketers home page has become one of our primary revenue streams for the site.

Trust the Journey and Adapt

You never know where you'll end up when you trust your heart and follow an idea. I didn't know in May of 1990 that one day I'd be the creator of IdeaMarketers.com and SheLovesGod.com or the author of 20 books. I didn't know I'd have a career that I absolutely adore — writing, speaking and promoting some of the most amazing people on the planet.

All I knew was that I wanted to be there for my kids and that I had an idea worth trying. I didn't wait until I had all my course materials created. I didn't wait until I'd researched the marketplace or even my competition. I just had a hunch that people would pay for private tutoring. And they did! What's more, when my students went on to get jobs, they told their employers about me. From there I got programming and consulting contracts with top notch companies. The experience was incredibly valuable. I was able to learn about business from some very savvy individuals as I went into companies and computerized their systems.

One of those gentlemen was a sales and marketing VP with a major corporation. He hired me to develop an Access database to track their sales. I learned a lot about marketing from this man that I would carry forward into my own marketing career.

Along your path, following your heart may take you on what looks like a major detour. It's like being on a road trip to your favorite vacation destination and feeling a strong impression to stop off and see the largest ball of twine. It may look like a silly waste of time, until you realize a piece of that twine comes in handy two-hundred miles down the road.

Some Ideas Need Time to Percolate

It's been my experience that my bigger ideas need time to simmer for a while. For example, the idea to do computer tutoring from home came at least a year or more before I needed to implement it. I'd rolled it around, thought of it, even considered my own method for teaching WordPerfect. Then when the strong impression came to implement that idea "right now," I took action immediately.

Our expert program at IdeaMarketers came in a similar fashion. I'd wanted to promote talented individuals and experts for a decade before I ever did it the way I envisioned. In fact, the original idea behind my purchase of the "IdeaMarketers.com" domain was to promote experts, but there was no traffic or content to make that happen. So when the article directory idea came along, I used the domain for that instead. In time, IdeaMarketers became a major web site with tons of traffic and content. Then, in 2007 when I wanted to promote experts again, it was an idea whose time had come. I implemented the system immediately, and the expert program took off.

Act Swiftly Upon the "Idea Whose Time Has Come"

When an idea strikes, and you have a strong impression to run with it, don't hesitate. Get going immediately, and do as much as you know how to do. Trust that the rest of the pieces will come. Start testing your idea to see if it works. I've seen lots of people think their ideas to death and spend months planning, only to miss important windows of opportunity and see their ideas fall flat. Until you put your idea out there, you don't really know whether anyone will "get it" or want it.

Once You Find Your Purpose, Let It Guide the Ideas You Pursue

If you're like me, you may have a gazillion ideas. I had a wonderful coach back in 2000 who used to say, "Just because you CAN make money doing it, Marnie, doesn't mean you should." Once I became clear about what I do — "highlighting truth and talent" — it became easier to know how to spend my time. I saw more clearly which ideas to pursue and which ones to dismiss.

For example, fifteen years ago, if someone had asked me to design an ecommerce web site for a shoe store, I would have taken the job. Today, I would decline, because it doesn't fit into the tagline of my life (highlighting truth and talent). Instead, I would refer the person to someone who could help them.

Twenty years ago, someone suggested I sell water filters. I did. It didn't work out. Now, I know why ... because selling filters didn't fit into my overall life purpose or message. I might buy the water filter now, but I wouldn't sell it.

It's liberating to be able to say "no" to things that take you off course and "yes" to the ideas that fit within your purpose. What's more, you'll be more successful and reap greater rewards when you stay focused on your purpose.

Create As You Go

It doesn't matter whether you have everything created yet. In fact, 90% of the time, I don't. I didn't have my course materials ready when I put the ad in the paper for computer training. There are lots of ways to buy yourself time. I booked people's appointments a couple weeks out. Not only did this give me more time to get ready, but it gave my students the impression that I was successful and already had clients.

Another way to create products and start selling them fast is to "drip" the content to your customers. Release your content over time as you create it. This works great for memberships where people pay you a monthly subscription. For example, when I created the "Abundance Quotient" course, I had recorded the bulk of the videos but didn't have them cleaned or ready for upload. I only had a couple of the lessons written that accompanied the videos. I went ahead and created the sales page and started selling the course for $7.95/month and dripped the lessons out to the people week by week as I created them.

Once I had 16 lessons created, I started selling them for a one-time payment instead of monthly payments. Customers received all 16 lessons at once to work through at their own pace. For that particular product, I tested and found that a one-time payment worked better than small monthly ones. People were willing to pay up front for all of it, and it was less technical maintenance on my end.

Keep Your Risks Low

Over the years I've watched people spend large amounts of time and money on ideas they didn't even know would work. One company, in particular, spent thousands of dollars developing an intricate web site that they had never tested on a small scale. A year and a half later and thousands of dollars in the hole, their investors cut funding. They had nothing left to market the web site. It never launched.

Had they tested it on a small scale and added features as they went, they could have proved to their investors that it was a viable idea and could have grown over time.

The key when you have an idea is to keep your risk low. For example, if you have an idea for a web site, don't purchase a dedicated server and pay high monthly hosting fees because you think your idea is going to take off. Just because you envision having so much traffic in a month or two that you'll be bursting at the seams doesn't mean you will. Few things take off that fast overnight. Select a hosting provider with whom you can grow. Keep your costs down, and let your hosting provider move you up as your business grows.

Whatever your idea is, get a prototype out there that doesn't cost a lot of money and test it. If you see interest, then you can develop and polish it to perfection over time.

The organic method for growing your business may seem slow, but it is more stable. "Slow and steady wins the race."

Remember You're Not Alone

Success is never created in a vacuum. You need other people to succeed. I would not be where I am today if it weren't for Alanna Webb and her generosity. Along my journey there have been friends, mentors, tutors, editors, subcontractors, joint venture partners and even critics who have helped me.

When it comes to implementing ideas, don't just look at what you know, but look at what other people know. Others are your resources. You may have to hire them, but you can get more inventive than that. You can barter services, too. My personal favorites are what I call "synergistic friendships."

Synergistic friendships are when heaven displays its match-making abilities to send individuals into your life who need what you have and who have what you need. When I meet someone like this and get to know them, I feel a distinct impression, "Help this person." It's a command I cannot deny nor keep from acting upon. I don't always know how or if that person will prove valuable to me. It really doesn't matter if they do. I've learned that if you put good things out, good things will come back to you — and not always from the person you helped. It's like pouring value into a river that flows back around to you.

This all became crystal clear to me in April of 2010, when I put together the *Light the World: Birthing Your Destiny Retreat* with two other presenters and two musicians. This event was a dream of a lifetime for me — an idea whose time had come. It brought together a message I feel compelled to share with incredible music and presentations. The women who came were amazing, eager to learn, and ready to serve others with their gifts. What's more, we were in one of my favorite places in the world — nestled amidst the orange mountains of Zion National Park. My favorite people, my favorite place, with cream of the crop participants coming together to share my heart's message — all synced with the most sublime soundtrack possible. Who could ask for more?

It was the second day of the event. I stood at the back of the room while the women were eating lunch, and I had this epiphany. Every one of the people on my team was there because I had followed my heart and the voice that told me, "Help that person." I followed that strong command-like impression as far back as six years earlier for the pianist to six months earlier for the violinist. All of these people came together to form an incredible team, ready and eager to make my dream a reality.

Remember what the legendary Zig Ziglar always says, "You can get everything in life you want if you will just help enough other people get what they want."

Sow good seeds. Put your best foot forward, seek to serve, and good things will come to you!

About Marnie Pehrson
Marnie is a best-selling author, speaker and online publicist who helps spiritually-minded entrepreneurs find their place in the world and deliver their messages online. She is the creator of the longest running content directory, IdeaMarketers.com, where you can promote your articles, press releases, information products, videos, audios and expertise. Marnie is also a wife and mother of 6 and the author of 20 fiction and nonfiction titles. If there's truth or talent to be highlighted, Marnie's your girl. Her mission is to help you live yours. Visit her online at MarniePehrson.com

If you'd like to build a business around your core passion, get the first 50 pages of Marnie's "You're Here for a Reason: Discover & Live Your Purpose" at http://www.IAmJoyful.com/purpose/

TAKE RESPONSIBILITY FOR YOUR LIFE

Adela Rubio

I've always been a dreamer. From the time I was a child, my internal world was much more familiar than the every day world of daily chores, school obligations and family expectations. I never played with dolls, though I had plenty of them. My favorite activity was to lie on my bed and dream. I would travel to make believe places, backwards and forwards in time. I would even play act some of my dreams, being a singer or a high priestess, especially when my brothers weren't around.

Very early I learned that I was different and a deep yearning for caring, connection and community was born. We emigrated from Cuba when I was a child. I grew up in an urban area experiencing the turbulent 60's of assassinations, race riots, the Vietnam War and Woodstock. To say that I was weaned on change and uncertainty is an understatement. But this constant change only strengthened the extraordinary dreamer in me. After all, change is a good thing, too, and the status quo is not insurmountable.

My earliest memory of "What do you want to be when you grow up?" was to be in the Peace Corps. I have always had a deep yearning to help, to serve, to make the world a better place. When I'd watch natural disasters on TV or see hungry children crying, it would hit me square in the heart. I have always felt an indelible connection to humanity at large. There is nothing that gives me greater joy than the expression and expansion of someone's potential. It's also been my own adventure, learning to explore and express my own potential.

Perhaps it is this deep-seated drive for self-expression that has made me question and challenge the rules. There's been a hearty, still small voice that has served me well over the years. I still remember my first message, "It doesn't have to be this way!" I've literally taken that as the mantra of my life. I have a history of trusting my heart, even when external circumstances indicate I have no grounds for it. Here are some of my more memorable moments.

I was 18 when I decided to audition for my college choir. I knew they required you to sight read, but I showed up anyway. At the start I let the director know, "I can't sight read, but I have perfect pitch and can sing anything by ear." I then proceeded to demonstrate. This isn't to say that I didn't hear the thoughts of, "Who do you think you are? You're not qualified. You don't meet the requirements." I did hear them, but there was a stronger pull within me, probably located between my heart and my belly, that propelled me to that audition and to speak boldly. I was the only member of the choir who couldn't sight read. It didn't make a difference.

I was a single mom in the '90's and temping at various law firms in New York City. I chose to temp because the freelance rates were better, and it gave me freedom to be with my small children. I wound up working for this one law firm a lot, and they invited me for a permanent position. I decided to take it. I had worked for most of the lawyers there and was well-liked and respected because I was fast, accurate and threw myself 100% into the work. I found out that the technology administrator was about to be fired, and they were looking to fill the position. I had no degree, no technical computer experience, in short, no qualifications for the job. I decided to go for it, citing that, "technical experience didn't mean that I didn't have technical acumen," and I pointed to my strong people skill set.

Well, it took some doing, but in the end the firm decided I was a good investment. They gave me the position and provided the training. Some of my friends said I had chutzpah. All I know is that *I knew I could do it*. The same voices still droned on, "You're not qualified. You don't have what it takes. Who do you think you are?" But something in my belly said, "Yes!" When I feel that force, that pull, it drives me and I can't not take the risk. It's too compelling!

Another 'trust your heart moment' occurred at the same law firm. While I was temping I had been taking musical theater classes, preparing to do a cabaret show in New York City. I didn't want to give that dream up, so I asked them if I could take my class on Tuesdays. I'd only be gone four hours, and I'd make good on the time I was out. It was an easy yes from the firm. No one had ever done it before, but they were willing and eager for me to have my show. Most of the law firm showed up for the show, too! The voices were still there, but a lot lighter by now. I knew to go for it because my body told me so.

My brother was the inspiration for my getting into shape in my early 30's. He had done amateur bodybuilding, and we often talked about opening up a gym. In the early 90's my brother found an investor and brought the dream to life. He offered me a position in the gym, but I asked to be a partner. I didn't have the money at the time, so I borrowed from a 401k and voila! I was a partner. Again, I judged what to do by the feel in my body. My excitement just shriveled up when he asked me to work at the gym, but being a partner had me ecstatic. Risking the no and daring the yes had become a part of my inner response.

We opened the health club while I was working at the law firm. Here I was with a full-time job managing technology for a New York City law firm and in the early mornings, evenings and weekends I worked at the gym. I became a certified fitness instructor, personal trainer and yoga teacher. I was in the best shape of my life and had more energy than I knew what to do with. It was at this time that the energy for the law firm was waning. I was about to turn 40 and had been doing a lot of personal development work. I was becoming very discouraged with the kind of work that we were supporting at the law firm. I wanted to contribute to life, and so I took another leap and left the law firm, with excellent salary benefits and security to run the health club. Everyone thought I was crazy. I was a success story at the firm - a no-degree, Hispanic woman holding a position in a male-dominated industry. My family and friends thought I was out of my mind. I had worked so hard to step into the position. I had 'made it.' They couldn't see that I was answering a higher call. The call of my heart and my vision.

I was pretty happy running the health club for a long time, but soon I got frustrated with why some people were successful in changing their bodies and others weren't. I decided to take some training with a holistic nutrition school in New York City to fill in the missing pieces of the wellness mystery. It was an extraordinary experience. Though the school billed itself as a nutrition school, it really was a school for transformation. I stayed there for two years and then traveled to India for training with a Zen Master. We travelled as a group, sixteen of us, and I experienced living in an aligned community. It was magical! I knew that this is what I wanted to create for myself and what I wanted to bring to the world. When I returned from my trip,

Trust Your Heart: Transform Your Ideas Into Income

I knew that I had to leave the family business and break out on my own. It was not easy at all. This was the hardest thing I have ever done in my life. It called into question my family values and long-held beliefs. In the end, the burning in my belly didn't leave, and I had to explore the next adventure - my own business.

It's taken me a number of years to put the pieces together, and I've had plenty more opportunities to trust my heart: leading a community at Coachville, leaving my marriage, focusing my business on community and partnership. Each time that I trusted my heart, it strengthened my ability to discern what's true. I won't tell you that I don't hear the voices anymore. I do. However, they are now portals to possibility. When I hear them, I say, "Yes!" Something juicy is up!" It hasn't always been easy to trust my heart, but every moment it's been worth it! The adventure has given me more rewards than I could have ever imagined, and I'm ready for more.

The most profound lessons that I have learned are ones that play out, not only in business, but also in my personal life. The greatest personal development program that I have ever experienced has been the launching of my business. Everything that stands in the way of your business also stands in your way. Further proof that separation is an illusion! There is no separation between your personal and business life. It's all an organic system. Wherever you go, there you are. The things that keep you from showing up brilliantly in your business are the very same things that are holding you hostage in your personal life. Here are the seven pivotal shifts that created quantum leaps in my business and my world.

1. Take responsibility for your life - all of it.

Here's the real secret to creating your own reality: Take responsibility for all of your life right now - the good, the bad, the beautiful. You create your own reality, even if you don't how you do it. If you're not conscious of what you're creating, then you're creating unconsciously. If you don't like what you've created, then make different choices. Before you can make an informed choice, you need to have an understanding of how you create. You create through your moment-by-moment, day-in day-out choices, which are based on your underlying thoughts and beliefs. Much of what you believe to be true, however, is actually what you have been trained to believe by your parents, your school, your church, even your TV programming. So really, what you consider to be 'your thoughts' are mostly programmed conditioning.

In order for things to change, your focus needs to shift from 'out there' to 'in here.' That's where your true power lies. Bring your attention to what goes on internally, and press the pause button so that you can choose your actions. This moving past your conditioned response is an ongoing adventure. It is your point of power, where you can engage your automatic judgments and assumptions. Here is where you can examine and curiously question your thoughts, feelings, and perceptions. It is this ongoing practice that will free you from a programmed life. You then have the power to change things. After all, that's how you create reality - with your choices. It is only in the living of a choice that you come to know what's true for you. Your life and business then become an authentic expression of you.

2. Expand your awareness with a writing practice.

Awareness is the first chain in the link from 'changing your thinking' to 'changing your world.' Einstein's thinking changed our world. You may not have considered this, but your thinking also affects the world. Your thoughts create your world — what's possible, what's not — and like a pebble tossed into a pond, they ripple into the world around you. How can you harness the power of your thinking by putting pen to paper?

Words are a snapshot in time. Like browsing through your family album, they capture and reveal your essence. Writing exposes the sweet, nectar-like core of your being with its vulnerable, sheer intimacy. A writing practice will help you glean these treasures.

Try this. Keep a pen and journal by your nightstand. Start writing when you awaken, as little as five minutes or as much as you like. Don't judge a thing. Just do a brain dump and release what wants to show up on the page. At the end of your writing, acknowledge three things in your life for which you are grateful.

Shifting your awareness from what's not working to what is working will create miracles in your life. Gratitude is a manifestation tool. Keep a notepad with you at all times. Inspiration will pop up at the most unexpected moments. Capture it! This practice alone will change your sense of self and what you believe is possible in your world.

3. Change is inevitable. Welcome it.

It's almost impossible to experience change and not feel the resistance to it. It's a natural response to the safety that you feel when you are in familiar territory. However, you don't shift your circumstances by staying in the comfortable and well-worn grooves. Change, although you may not always welcome it, is good news. It points to your next frontier.

What if you invoked your ability to move with life, instead of against it? What if instead of resisting change, you welcomed it? What if instead of avoiding the breakdown, you embraced the breakthrough?

The gap between where you are and where you want to be can be engaged powerfully. When things fall apart massively, it's a sign of huge potential. Notice how the great movements in history have been preceded by chaos and the disintegration of the dominant systems. What was seemingly 'bad news' gave rise to a new order.

Don't allow the surface layer of reality to dictate the depth of your vision. It is through your willingness to move with certainty and power through the uncharted landscape that a new opportunity has the ability to rise through you.

Things shift because you are compelled to push past the barrier of what you know into what you don't know. Usually there's a pretty compelling reason for this, too. You transform in the process, and thereby so does your world. And that's how everything changes. You are the engine of evolution!

4. Drop the drama and dogma. Find the empowering story.

All stories are of your own making. In rewriting the 'past' you open the portal to the power of your presence and awaken to the brilliance that is your true nature. The key shift here is in tapping into the potential of a situation, instead of the problem. If you focus on your current experience as a problem, it's very difficult to experience it from a positive perspective. Once you spiral into negative emotions, it's almost impossible to reorient around what's possible. If you don't shift how you feel about your life right now, your tomorrow will look exactly like yesterday!

Create stories that arise from your essence and inspire your actions. Judgment, assumptions, and resistance (your JAR) are powerful opportunities for transformation. They are invitations to an expanded awareness.

This is where your innate ability of story maker/story shaper comes in handy. You have the power to change the story whenever you choose. You always have the ability to shift your perspective and explore 'the story' from another point of view. When you do this, you will find that not only is there another perspective, but there are several available, all equally possible.

Notice which stories expand you and which ones diminish you. Rewrite the ones that diminish your sense of self and weave an empowering tale that you'll want to live into. Dance with life, instead of against life.

5. Celebrate everything and everyone.

Holidays, birthdays, anniversaries and achievements are moments marked for celebration. These events are littered throughout the year as times to honor and commemorate 'special occasions.' What if right now was a memorable moment? What if every moment is an opportunity to engage the 'more than' vs the 'less than' of life?

A common misperception is deriving your value and worth (and judging everyone else's) from the things that you do or have. What if you just lathered on the praise and took the opportunity to generously share acknowledgments in your personal and professional world? Most of the world is focused on pointing out what's wrong with you. What would happen if you entertained, on a regular basis, what's right with you instead of what's wrong with you? You will be amazed at the ripple of energy, ideas, relationships and more that will flow from this simple practice.

The energy of celebration makes you come alive. Take a moment to see what wants to be 'noticed' by you. In your seeing the beauty and abundance around you, you make it come alive. It doesn't matter whether it's a rock or a rose or a person. Your engagement of it organically creates presence and consciousness. Celebration is an alivening act, and abundance and joy are its natural by-products. Life then becomes an infinite celebration.

6. Embody the power of authentic partnership.

You're always in partnership, or relationship, to something or someone. The first element of partnership to explore is how you relate to yourself. After all, you can't relate to anyone or anything else in a way that is not congruent with who you are. You find out a lot about yourself when you are in relationship. Are you adding to or taking from? Are you shopping for a list of 'missing attributes' or wanting to collaborate with another? Are you relating out of habit or coming from your own abundance?

The playgrounds of relationship can be quite intense and full of illusion, and yet they are powerful opportunities for growth. Partnerships can be glorious adventures or heated battlegrounds. The first thing to understand is that people and things are locked in by your perception of them. Have you ever noticed that at the beginning of a relationship, personal or professional, that there's a sense of euphoria and all you sense is the promise of it? And that's all you find. Later on you start focusing on what's lacking, criticism wields its cruel grip and the partnership starts disintegrating.

What would happen if you freed every partnership from your expectations? What if you freed up everything to be what it IS and not what you'd like it to BE? What if you were transparent, from the very start, and focused how you could move that promise into a powerful partnership?

Here's a secret. Continue to focus and bring into being the promise of the partnership. Especially when there are challenges, witness the magnificence of your partner. It is the only thing that really changes people, from the inside out. Shift your perception and you will notice the person or circumstance change before your very eyes.

Gift your partnerships the freedom to be, unrestricted and relentlessly, true. Freeing the partnership transforms. All relationships serve you, but only when you are willing to free your unique essence and that of your partner's.

7. Connect and collaborate with a like-minded community.

My favorite Carolyn Myss quote sums up the power of community for me, "You evolve at the rate of your tribe." There is nothing that will catapult you and your business more rapidly than connecting and collaborating with a like-minded community. Whether you're thinking of social networks or joint ventures, the power of a resonant tribe is the new model for making things happen. There's no need to do it alone anymore. Link up to a like-minded tribe, and watch yourself and the community soar!

Many of you have been on a solo journey for far too long. Perhaps it's time to evaluate the lone wolf approach and upgrade your energy with an aligned community. Here are a few tips:

1. Make sure to **engage in activities that maximize your dominant natural abilities.** This seems pretty obvious, but you'd be surprised at how many times you'll say "Yes" to an activity or event that is not aligned with who you are. If you are a great listener, don't position yourself as the social coordinator.
2. **Choose or create social environments that energize your style of connection.** Some folks thrive on intimacy, some on an

audience. Know who you are and honor the essence of your nature.

3. **If you can't find a community that suits you, create it and host it.** Sometimes it seems like you just can't find 'your tribe' anywhere. Perhaps the call is not for you to 'find' the community but to 'create' the community. Take the leap and create the energy that you're seeking.

We're connective creatures by nature. A vibrantly aligned community will not only empower you, but will actually create transformation for everyone engaged in it. Take the lead and create a community that's worthy of your essence and expands the reach of your message.

Your work in the world plays itself out as your personal legend in the grand landscape of collective history. Who will you be and how will you play in the sandbox of time? Immerse yourself fully in the experience of your brilliance, and map out where and how you can put it into action! Create a passionate template that will launch your life adventure, and surrender yourself completely to your life's mission. Whether it's a business, an idea or a cause doesn't really matter. What's important is to launch the vision of what calls you into being, day after day.

Know that this spark is yours to bring into being. It's your responsibility to breathe the essence of your passion into your work. It's your persistence and insistence that will fan the flame of passion into reality. Be your passion, whatever is accessible to you now. In your living it, you bring it to life!

About Adela Rubio

Adela is a Conscious Business Mentor™ and Expert Tribe Builder who helps conscious entrepreneurs authentically articulate their essential message and build a profitable platform using the power of joint ventures and community. With five online telesummits under her belt, and more than 100 interviews with conscious business leaders, she is an expert at creating engaging and experiential online virtual events that position you as a thought leader while leveraging your talent, tribe, and technology. Visit her online at AdelaRubio.com

A Lover's Leap

Denise Wakeman

In 1996 at the age of 37, after an upheaval in my career, I found myself working as the manager of a small museum gift shop. It was a dead-end job. I was bored and uninspired and trying to figure out what was next for me. I was also in a new relationship with a charismatic and charming man with whom I had fallen in love.

Those two factors conspired to move me to make a major change in my life, and there was very little "head" involved in the decision. It was all heart. Now, I've taken this literally because I'm referring to the passionate heart, the heart of love. I trusted my heart and followed a path that took me to a place I could never have imagined and really, had never dreamed of…the place of entrepreneurship.

I took a leap of faith and uprooted myself from a secure, though dull, job, from my home, from my friends, from my family and moved from glorious, sunny Los Angeles to cold, wintery Ontario, Canada. There was a lot of "head" involved in the aftermath of the decision, but the decision was all heart. I took a huge risk, and I didn't do it pragmatically or come to my decision through a logical decision process.

It's a classic story. I met a man and fell in love. He was a Canadian living in Los Angeles. He, too, was in a transitional spot in his life and was ready to write a new chapter. After years in the construction business and years of study in many self-improvement models, he decided he wanted to start a business coaching practice. He asked if I wanted to join him on this new path. The idea was exciting to me. There was a caveat, though.

Robert had a farm property in rural Eastern Ontario, Canada. He was also in the middle of getting a divorce, which brought in lots of complications. He had followed his former wife to Los Angeles for her career advancement. He wanted to go back to Canada and bring his skills, his learning, and his education back to his home. That sounded like an adventure to me, and I was ready!

Leaving L.A. and moving to a new country was not a stretch for me. I had traveled a lot and lived in Europe for a couple of years right out of university. So the travel wasn't a problem.

The challenge for me was around how to start a business. I had been working in small businesses for a long time. I had managed art galleries and a retail bakery. I had some business sense, but that didn't come into play for some reason. We didn't approach the idea of starting a business with a lot of thought and care. I was caught up in the excitement of the adventure, and my attitude was, "Let's just figure it out as we go along." That's not exactly what I would recommend to anybody in hindsight.

- We did not research our niche.
- We did not develop a target market.
- We did not know if anyone was actually doing business coaching in Canada. (Coaching was a brand new profession in the U.S.)
- We did not have a suite of services or products.

And this is a biggie…we did not have any money (aside from a few hundred dollars in savings).

My passion and excitement meant I wasn't listening to my friends and my family. They were rather skeptical about the whole insane idea. They didn't know Robert well. We hadn't been together that long -- 5 to 6 months. I was giving up a condo I had just bought a couple years before. I was giving up a secure job with benefits. The only person I would know in Canada was Robert.

I was only listening to the passion of my heart. I wanted to be with this man. It sounded fun and exciting. I was ready to try something different and new rather than going with the same J-O-B year after year. I was in my mid 30's and uninterested in having low paying jobs anymore.

In reality, I'm usually a pragmatic, thoughtful person. I'm not flighty. I'm steady and determined and though I love adventure, I tend to think things through before taking massive action.

Looking back, I think it was the possibility of creating something for the first time ever. It would be mine in partnership with this other person. I wasn't going to be an employee. It was a chance to see if I could do that. I didn't know. I had only had jobs before. I felt I was at a point in my life where I didn't have anything to lose. Sure, I owned a condo. So what? I ended up losing it because I couldn't rent it for as much as I owed. But in the end, that didn't matter.

I had everything to gain. Although, at the time, I didn't realize how much I would be learning about myself. Once the decision was made and we started moving forward, it was not easy, and I felt plenty of anxiety and fear. We were so unprepared.

We had many challenges. Not only did we have to figure out our young relationship, we had to learn what it meant to have a business, and figure out how to educate our potential clients whose definition of coaching related to hockey. Also, we had very little in the way of technology. We had one dial-up phone line. We were out in the middle of nowhere on 100 acres, 45 minutes from any town. And we had no money. Really, we were not pragmatic about this at all. If I had listened to my head and thought this through, I would not have left Los Angeles.

I definitely felt some fear. I had sold almost everything I owned and shipped or packed the rest into the van. I really freaked out about a day and a half into the drive from Los Angeles to Toronto.

I looked at this guy and thought, "Do I know this person well enough to do this? I don't even know if I'll be able to get in to Canada. And if I do get across the border, will I be able to stay?" I was unprepared and just flying high on love and excitement.

On the other hand, my pragmatic side urged me to keep moving forward. I'm not the kind of person to say, "Okay, I quit. Turn around. Take me home."

And I am smart enough to know that if it didn't work after I got there, I could get on a plane and come home. I could just start over and find a job. I also knew that my family would embrace me and help me and not beat me up if things didn't work out.

I found myself in Canada at the beginning of winter.

I won't go into any more of the many obstacles we faced. Just know that despite the numerous challenges, we did persevere and built a six-figure business over the next few years.

Upon our arrival at the farm, the head kicked in and we worked very hard to learn what we needed to know and to get by with little until things turned around. My logical nature took over.

Getting through ignorance was a matter of spending a lot of time doing research on the Internet. Tapping into the few contacts we had was essential as well. Swallowing pride and asking for loans from family was tough, and despite the skeptics who thought we couldn't do it, every person got paid back.

"Don't wait until everything is just right. It will never be perfect. There will always be challenges, obstacles and less than perfect conditions. So what? Get started now. With each step you take, you will grow stronger and stronger, more and more skilled, more and more self-confident and more and more successful." ~Mark Victor Hansen

The quote by Mark Victor Hansen sums up my situation perfectly. It's a philosophy I still adhere to for the most part, though usually *after* I make a decision to pursue a project or idea!

A crucial part of moving from this particular dream to a successful, thriving coaching practice was discipline and focus. Once settled, we focused on what we wanted to create. Then we found the resources and experimented.

Experimentation is critical because it's impossible to know what will work when you're starting down a new path in a new industry. I took classes and modeled what leaders in the industry were doing. I tried out a lot of marketing tactics to find what would work for our business in our geographic location.

And every step of the way, we were adjusting and tweaking, learning, applying and testing. For example, we quickly learned that someone would not engage in a coaching program until they got a sample. Especially since most of our local prospects had no idea what coaching was or how it could benefit them.

We adapted to telephone coaching very quickly when we realized we could extend our reach to the U.S. and other countries. Once we had a website, it became clear we were not limited. In fact, the phone was preferable since we lived so far from any towns, and the ones we were near didn't match our target audience.

Ultimately we did **build a successful coaching practice.** Sadly, our marriage ended and I moved back to Los Angeles. However, every single thing I learned in the six years I lived in Canada enabled me to grow into an even more successful business woman. Everything I learned, I was able to apply when I had to start over again.

Each lesson helped me to step out from behind the scenes, supporting my husband, and become the star of my own successful business...**the revenues of which have far exceeded** what I generated with my former husband.

Despite the tough times and anxiety at the outset, I am grateful for that experience and that I listened to my heart at that moment and not my head.

Lessons Learned

Sometimes you don't have a choice. When you're passionate about your idea, no matter how crazy *others* think it is, sometimes you have no choice but to make it work. Maybe you have to for financial reasons or because you've made a commitment to others, or you simply must do it to prove to yourself that you can.

For me, we were in a situation where we had to make something work. There was no back up, no Plan B. This meant that we could not mess around. We had to hit the ground running.

I generally recommend having a Plan B. For example, when I returned to Los Angeles, I found myself starting over again. Being in a state of shock about the sudden end of my marriage, I immediately got a J.O.B. That didn't last long. After six years of running my own business, being an employee didn't suit me. Based on my experience, I knew I could start a new business. This time, however, I gave myself a time line – six months – and I had enough savings to support myself for those six months if I did not get one single paying client. Fortunately, I engaged two clients within a month and never looked back.

You don't always get to have all the resources you want. Depending on the idea you want to implement and where you are in your business, you may not be able to afford or have access to the ideal resources. You have to **adapt and use what you've got** until you can afford to invest in better tools or help.

In 1996, the Internet was just hitting its stride as a commercial tool. That was great since we lived in a remote area, and it enabled us to reach more people. However, we had only one dial-up phone line. That meant we had to negotiate who would use the line – Robert for coaching and prospecting calls, then me on the Internet for marketing and research. Logistically, because of where we lived, we couldn't get a second line installed even if we had the thousands of dollars it would have cost, because we were a mile in from the main road and phone lines. That was an interesting challenge until we moved to Ottawa, the capital of Canada, and finally had access to a high speed Internet line.

Do your research. Nothing beats learning about your area of interest. Generally this is good to do before you dive in, but if your decision was made with your heart before the head took over, that's OK. Start now.

I spent hours on the Web (this was before Google, too!) doing a lot of research about coaching, business coaching, and executive coaching. I started finding people doing the same thing. I started following people who were blazing the trail in the coaching industry. While we were somewhat at the leading edge in Canada, we definitely weren't the advanced crew.

Document what you're learning and put it into practice!

Model the leaders. I was following the leaders, but I didn't stop there. Implementation is everything when you're in the "idea to income" phase. When you discover a strategy or tactic that is working for someone else in your industry, study it and figure out how you can adapt it to your idea.

In 1997, teleseminars were a novelty. I started attending teleseminars on a regular basis, not only to learn the new skills I needed to build my business, but to study how to do teleseminars.

Now, of course, you can't get through a day without getting an invitation for a teleseminar, telesummit or webinar. But in the late 1990's, they were the hot new thing, and one had to rent a conference line by the hour. Now, tools like InstantTeleseminar.com make it super easy to set up, manage and produce a teleseminar for 2,000 people with a minimal investment. This one tool helped transform our fledgling, local business into one with a global clientele.

There comes a time when you have to make an investment. While it may not always be the case, money may be in short supply when you're implementing a new idea. However, sometimes, you've got to bite the bullet and make the investment. You've got to invest in training or consulting or in getting help to implement your idea.

Before heading to Canada, we invested in a consulting session with a coach in L.A. who had a successful practice. He graciously agreed to meet with us and shared tips about how to get started, types of coaching packages we should consider offering, how to book clients, and tools to use with clients. Even though we didn't have a lot of spare cash, this was an important investment that enabled us to skip a couple of steps. You don't have to reinvent the wheel. Invest in your own coach or mentor or expert who has walked the path before you. Even an hour of consulting advice can accelerate your progress.

Today, I mentor other service professionals on how to build a powerful presence on the Web. And I continue to work with my own mentors to make sure I stay on top of my personal, professional and business development and growth.

Most everything you learn can be applied to your next big idea. If the implementation of your idea takes you into new territory, be confident that what you're learning will come back to support you in future endeavors.

While I did struggle in the early stages of starting the coaching practice, everything I learned and studied - all the trial and error of finding ways to connect with people, website building, email list building, and figuring out what the heck an autoresponder was - it all served me when I started a new business on my own.

What I realized after my husband and I parted company 6 years later is that I had a strong foundation to create my own business.

The vision of who you are may change quite radically. When you achieve your goal, when your idea turns into income, shift happens. There's nothing like success to build confidence, and with confidence comes the passion to go for your next idea.

Previously, I had been happy to work in the shadows. I had never wanted to be in the spotlight. But when things changed in my life again, I realized I had grown to the point where I could step out into the spotlight and be the star of my own show. I had created a successful business once; I could do it again and didn't need anyone else to do it. This was a huge shift for me. I understood and was very confident about what I could accomplish and that I could do it again.

A key element to developing this attitude of confidence is to remind yourself how far you've come. Once in a while you've got to look back down the mountain to see what you've achieved, rather than solely focus on how far you still have to go to get to the top. Your achievements are the fuel to take you to the top. And don't listen to the naysayers. Their negative energy won't support your dream.

What does this all mean? While I learned a tremendous amount about the nuts and bolts of how to build a service-based business, the most profound lessons go beyond the technical and logistical elements of starting a business.

As I have pondered and relived that seminal time of my life, the tools and tactics, while important, are not what shaped me. What I have realized is that my willingness to take a risk and go with a dream, ended up serving me very well. If I had listened to the voices – both internal and external – telling me I was making a mistake or the idea was crazy, I wouldn't be where I am today…a successful, respected online marketer and entrepreneur.

About Denise Wakeman
Denise is a Business Blogging and Online Visibility Expert. Denise was an early online marketer and has been using the Internet with great success as a marketing tool since 1996. She is an expert at helping authors, speakers, service professionals, and small business owners leverage blogs for their business, as well as strategically use social media tools to boost online visibility to get more traffic, leads, clients and opportunities. Denise writes on two marketing blogs, is a columnist for SocialMediaExaminer.com and is a contributing author on business blogging in "Success Secrets of Social Media Superstars." Visit her online at www.DeniseWakeman.com.

THE WINDING PATH

Stephanie Chandler

In 2002 I was selling software in the Silicon Valley, which included a $4 million quota, a relentless schedule, and a hefty paycheck. That year I attended a sales conference in Las Vegas, something we were required to do quarterly. At that particular event, I was hosting one of my clients—an executive from a major Dot Com. We went out to dinner and then headed into the casino. I sat down at a blackjack table, took two sips from a cocktail, and the next thing I knew, I was on the floor.

Yep. I had fainted on the floor of a Las Vegas casino.

If you need medical attention, you get a lot of it - really fast - on the floor of a casino. There was a posse of people standing over me, including medics, security guards, and casino staff dressed in suits. No doubt they were also concerned that I was pulling an Oceans 11 on the place, but that wasn't the case at all.

I had been feeling ill for months, but instead of taking time out to see a doctor, I actually carried a bottle of Maalox™ in my briefcase. I remember pulling in to park at a client's office and taking a swig straight from the bottle before heading in to meetings. Thanks to the

Vegas incident, I learned I had a bleeding ulcer. That was the year I turned 30, and it became clear that a major lifestyle change was in order.

I began planning my exodus from corporate America, but didn't know what to do next. I kept coming back to the fact that I had always wanted to be a writer. Since I didn't yet know how to make a living doing that, I settled on what I thought was the next best option: I decided to open a book store.

A year later I had written a whopping 42-page business plan, signed a lease, and opened a 2800-square-foot book store in Sacramento, California. When I quit my job, my family and friends thought I had lost my mind. I had traded in a $4 million quota to sell $4 paperbacks. My plan was to build a passive income business so I could write novels from the back office. Looking back, I can see how that might have seemed a little crazy.

About six weeks after I opened the store, I looked around and thought, "Oh, no! What have I done?" I didn't want to run a retail business. After barely sitting at a desk for years, I was suddenly chained to the business, day in and day out. I felt like a prisoner. I didn't like most of the tasks involved: hiring, firing, inventory management, customer issues, and middle-of-the-night alarm company calls. The only tasks I enjoyed were marketing the business and figuring out ways to increase website traffic.

At the same time, I realized I lacked the imagination needed to be a novelist, yet I still had an intense desire to write. I was also receiving a steady stream of calls and visits from my Silicon Valley peers. Many expressed that they wished they'd had the courage to do what I did. They wanted to leave their jobs behind but didn't think it was possible.

Then I read a quote by Toni Morrison:

"If there is a book that you want to read, but it hasn't been written yet, then you must write it."

I had read dozens of business start-up books, but none had answered all of my questions about the realities of starting a business. So I decided that I would write the book that I wanted to read—one that might inspire some of my friends and help them realize that there could be life after corporate America.

I got to work on my first book, a business start-up guide. I attended the San Francisco Writer's Conference with a hefty book proposal in hand and generated a lot of interest from literary agents and publishers, but the rejection letters soon followed.

One day I received a call from Mike Larsen, a well-known agent in San Francisco. He told me he liked my work, but that I needed a platform. He said that big publishers wanted authors with a built-in audience. "You need to be out speaking to thousands of people each year." When I pointed out that what he was suggesting was like putting the cart before the horse, and that I would be able to book speaking engagements and build a following *after* I had a book published, he told me it was a challenge I had to solve. Without an audience, he couldn't help me.

That was life-changing advice, for which I will always be grateful.

Since I had just left the rat race and wasn't ready to embark on a whole new career as a road warrior, I decided to investigate options on the internet. I knew there had to be a way to reach an audience without getting on a plane. I decided to launch a website targeted toward business owners and aspiring entrepreneurs, and BusinessInfoGuide.com was born. I shared resources and website links and began writing articles. I learned about search engine optimization (SEO) and explored places on the internet where I could promote the site. I sent out an electronic newsletter, and the first edition went out to a grand total of eight subscribers (today that list is in the thousands). I was figuring things out as I went along and having a great time putting the puzzle together.

After growing impatient with the publishing pursuit, I decided to self-publish my book, *The Business Startup Checklist and Planning Guide*. I listed it for sale on BusinessInfoGuide.com a full two months before it was in print—and that darn book started selling immediately. That's when I understood what Mike Larsen meant when he said I needed a platform. I had built an audience that was interested in what I had to say.

Soon after, I decided that I wanted to sell special reports and e-books. I looked for a book on how to create and sell products, and there wasn't one available, so I studied how others were selling their information products. I assembled my first products and listed them on the site. They also began selling immediately.

Can you guess what I did next?

I wrote a book called *From Entrepreneur to Infopreneur: Make Money with Books, eBooks and Information Products*, and I submitted proposals to exactly two publishers. A month later I had a book contract with John Wiley and Sons. Because I had an audience, a high-traffic website, and some success with my self-published book, getting a publishing deal seemed easy in comparison to my previous attempt.

From there, momentum grew and my new career took on a life of its own. I was receiving requests for media interviews, invitations for speaking engagements, and consulting contracts. I ended up signing with a literary agent who sold two subsequent books for me: *The Author's Guide to Building an Online Platform* (Quill Driver Books/Linden Publishing) and *LEAP! 101 Ways to Grow Your Business* (Career Press).

In the midst of all of this, I sold the bookstore. I was hardly ever there, and it was a great relief to let go of that responsibility. I also launched a marketing business and worked with clients all over the country.

Then one day I realized that I was constantly talking to aspiring authors who were overwhelmed by the prospect of self-publishing. Some had gone down that path only to end up disappointed with the sub-par results (something I call the self-publishing "do-over"). Others wanted to produce professional results and were wary of the big subsidy publishers (I call them "author factories"). Everyone needed help with marketing.

After identifying the need in the market for high-quality self-publishing assistance, along with my own experiences and a desire to help authors achieve their goals, I morphed my marketing business into a custom publishing company in 2008 (Authority Publishing). We specialize in business, self-help, memoir and other non-fiction books. Despite the recession, growth has been phenomenal, and it has been incredibly satisfying to help other authors achieve their dreams.

In addition to being CEO of Authority Publishing, today I continue my work as an author and speaker. It has been a wonderful journey. I often look back on the past eight years and reflect on the winding path that brought me to this place — doing work that I love and that I believe I was meant to do. It all started with the idea that I wanted to write. And the rest came from being curious, learning, uncovering opportunities, and not being afraid to pursue them.

I call myself a "Silicon Valley Refugee." I don't miss anything about having a job. I decide how many hours I work each day, which clients I want to work with, which team members I want to hire, and how business gets done.

If an entrepreneur tells you that running a business is easy, he's lying! It's not. There have been many difficult days. But I'm grateful for all of it, especially the difficult times, because I have learned something new at every turn. And it all started by taking the first step on a path that I thought was clear, with a route that changed during the journey.

Early on, the book store seemed like a gigantic mistake. But looking back, that wasn't the case at all. It was the first stepping stone along the journey. It served as a remarkable training ground for running a business, dealing with employees and payroll, marketing online and offline, and building a solid business that I could ultimately sell. The whole experience led me to write books and launch my publishing business. There was no way I could have walked away from the Silicon Valley and do what I do today. I had to take the journey.

And you know what? I wouldn't change a thing.

Lessons from the Winding Path

I could write a whole book about the lessons from my journey (in fact, I've written six books to date!). Here are some of the top lessons I've learned along the way.

Trust Your Heart: Transform Your Ideas Into Income

1. Don't Be Afraid to Chart a Different Course

If I had stuck with my initial plan, I'd be miserable right now. I imagine myself sitting in the back office at the book store, a frustrated novelist, watching the clock. When I had doubts early on, I didn't tell a soul—not even my husband. How could I admit such a big mistake? But instead of dwelling on what felt like an impossible situation, I changed my course. I stayed open to new possibilities and took some calculated risks.

2. Find Lessons Everywhere

I learned so much in those early years, and many of those lessons carried forward into helping me run my business today. For example, I only hire really great people. If I can't find "really great," I keep looking. The point is that just about everything you do includes a lesson you can carry forward on your journey. I also use skills learned during my time in the Silicon Valley. No time spent is ever wasted if you find the lesson.

3. Find a Way to Make Your Passion Pay

If you don't know what your passion is, find it. And if you do know what it is and you aren't doing work that you are passionate about, find a way to change that. My passion will always be writing, and I've discovered many other things I love to do in addition to that (like teaching and speaking). I don't spend 8 hours a day working with my passion, but it is a huge part of what I do every day, which makes life so much more satisfying. Figure out how to incorporate passion into your work life, and it will never feel like work.

4. Write a Book

I had no idea the opportunities that I would uncover after writing a book. Being an author has opened countless doors. It is also a legacy that you leave behind, a tool for business growth, and a wonderfully satisfying accomplishment. If you're one of those people who thinks you want to write a book "someday," don't put it off. You'll be so glad you didn't wait.

5. Build a Support Network

I've noticed a theme throughout my entrepreneurial journey, and that is in the power of community. I have been involved in numerous trade associations where I aligned with fellow members and found a place to commiserate and share experiences. Today I'm involved with a mastermind group, which is like having a really cool board of directors. Ten of us get together for a full day each month and brainstorm ideas for our respective businesses. (Note that my group is something I created, and not something that anyone is paying to be involved in. It's a group of smart people who share mutual respect for each other.)

Being an entrepreneur can be lonely. You don't have coworkers or many people who understand what you do. If you do nothing else, bring together a group of smart people who can help you think through decisions, develop goals, and move your business to the next level.

6. Never Stop Learning

My personal goal is to learn something new every day. If you never build on your knowledge, you risk staying stuck in the same place. There are many, many ways to learn.

- Study industry blogs and websites
- Read books (I read at least one per week.)
- Take classes
- Subscribe to trade publications
- Discover golden nuggets via social media
- Participate in trade associations
- Attend educational conferences and events
- Spend time with smart people
- Find a mentor

7. Get a Great Notebook

You've heard the advice about writing a business plan, and I do believe in them because they force you to think through important details. However, most plans change - often. My best business plan is a leather-bound journal (it's a Circa™ by Levenger™) that I carry everywhere. I jot down ideas, sketch out plans for new services and products, and keep all of my thoughts organized. Next to my computer, it is my best business tool.

8. Keep Your Finances in Check

I remember the first week in my bookstore and the struggles I had trying to understand QuickBooks™. I have always hated accounting and anything to do with math, so I immediately realized I needed to hire help. If you don't have a bookkeeper and good accountant, you could be missing out. Not only can they help keep finances in check, they are there for you if you need extra help or guidance. I was audited by the IRS several years ago and without a pro at my side, I would have been a mess (I'm not the most organized person and would have shown up with a shoebox full of receipts). Thanks to her ongoing work on my books and receipt tracking, I walked out of the audit with no adjustments. And by the way, in recent years the IRS has increased its number of audits, especially on small businesses, so it's best to be prepared.

9. Spend Money to Make Money

I see so many entrepreneurs clinging to every dime that they earn. But you have to invest money in your business on marketing campaigns, labor, website management, accounting, software, quality computers and phone systems, and much more. Set aside 20% of what you earn, and invest it toward business growth. I'll bet you will be surprised by the difference this makes.

10. Don't Work Too Hard

Okay, the reality is that most entrepreneurs work around the clock in the early years. This is often what it takes to get a business to the profitable stage. But once that happens, do yourself a favor and scale it back. Entrepreneurs often report finding it difficult to balance work and family. I know, because I share these struggles. But I also know that I can't take my business with me when I go, and that I don't want to miss out on creating memories with my kids. Make your family and your health a priority, and put systems in place so that you can put in an 8-hour day (instead of 12-hours!), take an afternoon off when you want to, and take a vacation. You've earned it!

About Stephanie Chandler

Stephanie is an author of several books including *LEAP! 101 Ways to Grow Your Business, From Entrepreneur to Infopreneur: Make Money with Books, eBooks and Information Products* and *The Author's Guide to Building an Online Platform: Leveraging the Internet to Sell More Books*. Stephanie is also founder and CEO of www.AuthorityPublishing.com, which specializes in custom publishing for non-fiction books, and BusinessInfoGuide.com, a directory of resources for entrepreneurs. A frequent speaker at business events and on the radio, she has been featured in *Entrepreneur Magazine, BusinessWeek, Inc.com, Wired* magazine and many other media outlets.

SHOESTRING MARKETING

Jessica Swanson

I wouldn't change a thing about my life now – but of course while I was on the journey, I wasn't always so sure. When I went to college directly after high school, I hadn't given much thought to what I was going to do with my life. I enrolled in the English education program, obtained my high school teaching certificate and at twenty-two, I married Brad, my high school sweetheart, and secured a high school English position in the Chicago suburbs. We had a sweet, little one-bedroom apartment just a few blocks from my school and "real-life" had begun.

For the next eleven years, I followed the path without deep thought about how much I really liked what I was doing. I acquired a Master's Degree in Written Communications and eventually added consulting and public speaking to my repertoire. Three children followed, and there wasn't much time to evaluate my career. I loved my students. I loved helping apathetic students grow into enthusiastic writers. I loved watching indifferent students grow into life-long readers. But I wasn't passionate about the work I did. I truly had it all. I was happily married with three amazing children and a great job, but one that didn't excite me. But what could I do? I had a mortgage, bills and commitments just like everyone else. So I continued to follow this path.

In retrospect, teaching in a high school environment was not a perfect match for my personality. I was fiercely independent, extremely self-motivated and flourished in situations where I could lead. Even though I had chosen a safe and secure path of teaching, I didn't blossom through safety and security. Yes, I loved my students, but I wasn't cut out for bosses, difficult colleagues, strict work schedules governed by bells and the political red-tape that comes with a teaching job. I especially disliked being evaluated by supervisors who knew less than I did.

One day, everything in our lives came to a screeching halt. Our middle daughter, Claire, who was five years old, was diagnosed with leukemia. In the blink of an eye, our whole world tumbled down. Claire needed intense treatment, and consequently, I decided to teach part-time. For the next six months the hospital was my second home. Claire underwent intensive chemotherapy, spinal taps, bone marrow aspirations, blood transfusions and two port surgeries. I never missed a single treatment.

My sweet little Claire was weak, sick and spent most of her mornings throwing up before leaving for kindergarten. In a few short weeks, she was swollen and bloated because of large doses of steroids and lost all of her curly, blond hair. But, throughout her horrendous ordeal, she never complained and continued to sing, dance and smile. She still remains my heroine to this very day.

While Claire's fight for her life required extra care and attention, I also needed to make sure that my other two children knew they were loved and secure and they didn't feel left out. For the next three years, my life was dedicated to my family. The hardest challenge that I had ever experienced forced me to reevaluate my life. I discovered that life is about embracing what makes us happy. If there are difficult circumstances within our control, we can change them; in fact, we must change them.

This sobering episode made me feel adamant that I wanted to spend more time with my family, but I knew I wanted to work at a job that I loved. I quit teaching in order to find a more "flexible" career and began my real estate renovation career. Brad and I purchased an apartment in the city with the hopes of "fixing" it up and reselling it for a profit. That, as it turned out, was not a good plan. We hired a plumber to "winterize" the house and turn off all of the water. Unfortunately, the plumber didn't *quite complete his work.* One cold winter day, the water wasn't entirely shut off, the frozen pipes burst and the entire apartment was instantly destroyed. Our insurance company refused to pay for it, so we were left with an uninhabitable house and a daunting $225,000 mortgage.

Even though I was devastated, I knew I couldn't quit now. I had hit a brick wall, but I needed to find a way around it. I focused on my strengths, decided to write a book and develop an online membership site devoted to the one topic for which we all search: happiness. I wanted to share my own personal story of adversity and help others understand that happiness can be learned. I had created my very first business, "Happiness University." I spent almost every waking moment writing my book and building the membership site. Once it was completed, I had found my passion. I believed that my program could change lives.

However, like so many small business owners, I had no idea how to get the word out about my small business. I didn't know anything about marketing except that I knew that marketing was the key to any small business success. If I couldn't find prospects, I couldn't make sales. If I couldn't make sales, I would fail.

My daughter was recovering from a life-threatening illness. I had quit my job, we were deeply in debt, and I was the owner of a business that I had no idea how to market. This was one of the bleakest times in my life. These were the times that I felt like giving up. There were days that I didn't know what to do next. I knew that others depended on me, so I continued to move forward and put one foot in front of the other.

As I look back on this difficult time in my life, I realize that our dismal financial situation forced me to work harder. Building my small business couldn't be a hobby or an amusing past-time. For the sake of my family I had to succeed and move us from our current situation. If I hadn't had bill collectors on my back, I wouldn't have worked so hard.

I set off on an intense learning expedition and spent thousands of hours studying everything that I could find on marketing. I had very little money, and I soon found that my options were limited. I couldn't run expensive pay-per-click (PPC) campaigns. I wasn't able to buy internet banner ads. I didn't have the funds to launch full-fledged magazine advertising campaigns or weekly newspaper ads. I needed different solutions. I turned my research to "free marketing." To my surprise, there was very little to be found on this topic. There were some bits and pieces, but not a solid formula or program for a small business owner on a very limited budget. I often joke, that over the course of three years, I earned a "Virtual PhD" in Shoestring Marketing Strategies.

This was the turning point of my life. Everything came together for me, and Shoestring Marketing was born. My concept was to help entrepreneurs, on a shoestring marketing budget, learn the needed skills and strategies to market their own businesses. Shoestring Marketing allowed me to use all of my past experiences in my current career. I tapped into my teaching background, drew upon my love of writing, accessed my curricular talents, while helping others learn complicated strategies in a straight-forward manner.

This is my life, my passion, and I wouldn't change a thing about the circumstances that brought me to this point. Ten years ago, I had no idea that I would be the owner of a successful small business. In fact, it never even occurred to me. Today Claire is a happy, healthy 14-year old, my small business is thriving and I love my work. I am happy and content, but there were very tough times to get to the point where I am today. I know now that all the difficult events in my life caused me to make the necessary decisions to create a life of passion and success.

Ten Marketing Lessons for Small Business Owners on a Shoestring Marketing Budget

There are several marketing lessons that you should know to catapult your business to the top. If your goal is to be a master marketer, several principles follow that you will need to understand and implement.

1) You don't need to spend money to make money.

In terms of marketing, there has never been a better time for small business owners. Ten years ago, small business owner had few options when it came to marketing. They could use newspaper ads, magazine ads, direct mail, radio or television. These were expensive avenues and many small business owners did not have the capital to follow these paths.

With the onset of the internet and social media platforms (such as Facebook, Twitter and LinkedIn), there are now hundreds of places to market your business on a shoestring budget. The best news is that many of these free marketing platforms work better than paid marketing platforms because the small business owner is able to develop enduring relationships with their prospects, clients and customers. Take heart that you can market your business for little to no-cost while reaping huge rewards in the process.

2) We are all on equal footing.

Many years ago, small business owners couldn't compete with big businesses when it came to marketing. Obviously, running a multi-million dollar commercial during the SuperBowl was inconceivable. However, the marketing world has changed. Now, any small business owner can easily and quickly develop a presence on Facebook and Twitter. Even the tiniest business can host a blog and submit a press release.

Like many other parts of our society, marketing is now flat. We are living in exciting times where small business owners can promote their businesses alongside Fortune 500 companies. Even better, the small business owner has a decided advantage over the large organizations. Small businesses lack heavy bureaucratic layers and can make marketing decisions instantly, change directions quickly and create important relationships with their prospects faster and more efficiently than larger, bulkier businesses.

3) Flaunt your uniqueness.

In the marketing world you can create your Unique Selling Proposition (USP). This is the indispensable identity of your small business. With small business competition at a premium, small business owners need to clearly differentiate themselves within their industry.

Your clients and customers need a compelling reason to do business with *you* as opposed to all the others who are clamoring for their attention. You must prove to your prospects that you are the exclusive "go-to" person in your industry.

4) Identify your ideal client or customer.

Many small business owners make the mistake of marketing to the masses. The problem with this approach is that it makes it impossible to differentiate yourself. It also dilutes your marketing message and isn't cost-effective. Instead, you need to identify, as specifically as possible, your ideal client or customer. Once you know who you are marketing to, you will design your marketing efforts with your ideal client in mind. You will connect with them, relate to them and bond with them. When your prospects feel as if you understand their issues and appreciate their efforts, they are more likely to do business with you.

5) Recognize that you are a problem-solver.

Your prospects are constantly searching for solutions to their most pressing problems. They are on a constant quest to be richer, thinner, happier or more intelligent. They are looking for short-cuts, quick-fixes and speedy solutions. You need to pinpoint the unique problems that your customers and clients face.

Once you've identified their problems, you can convince them that your particular product or service provides the best solution. Your belief in your product or service will be motivating and persuasive. Your prospect should feel no need to look elsewhere. You are the solution for which they have been searching.

6) Create a landing page.

Most small business owners understand the importance of a web-presence in today's marketplace. However, small business owners who create a landing page that asks prospects to supply their names and emails (in exchange for a valuable free offer) are able to build an email list. A list of prospects who are interested in you and your small business is a valuable starting point for all small business owners.

Asking prospects to sign up for your free newsletter is not appealing. To build a robust list of interested prospects, you need to create a tantalizing free offer that your prospects simply can't refuse. You can craft a downloadable e-book or special report, send them a series of instructional videos or create an audio class. Your free offer should be designed to give your prospects a taste of your product and services.

7) Create massive visibility.

In today's fast-paced world, your prospects need to see your marketing message up to *twenty-seven times* before they even notice you. That's why you should create a dominant presence on a variety of marketing platforms. If your prospects read your Tweets, view your Facebook updates, read your online articles and watch your YouTube video, they can't help but notice you. You want your prospects exclaim, "I see her everywhere! Who in the world is she?" The natural next step is for them to find out more about your small business, visit your landing page and download your valuable free offer.

8) Educate. Don't sell.

Once your prospects join your "list," you need to nurture that relationship. A prospect needs to like, trust and ultimately learn from you before they are ready to make a purchase. This is the time to send them educational tips, tools and strategies from your industry including: articles, videos, podcasts, blog posts and press releases. Education is the fastest way to capture your prospects' hearts.

9) Treat your customers like royalty.

Don't make the common mistake of forgetting about your current customers. Too often, small business owners make the sale and mistakenly think that their job is done. Your current customers and clients are a priceless part of your overall success. Treat them with a bit of extra TLC by paying extra attention to them, giving them special offers and discounts and rewarding those who are loyal. When you treat your customers well, up to 30% will purchase from you again.

10) Be consistent and patience.

The final and most important piece of advice for anyone launching a marketing campaign is to be consistent and have patience. Good marketing doesn't happen overnight. In order for marketing to be effective, your prospective customers must see your brand over and over again. Make a promise to yourself that you will be patient and consistent in your marketing efforts. Those that do realize this reap huge rewards in their business.

Again, all ten Shoestring Marketing lessons are important to your business success. When you understand and implement these secrets, your small business will quickly rise to the top of its industry.

About Jessica Swanson

Jessica has helped thousands of small business owners, all over the world, implement low-cost, high-impact DIY marketing campaigns. Armed with years of teaching and a M.S. in Written Communications, Jessica takes complicated marketing concepts, turns them upside-down, and makes them incredibly simple and outrageously straightforward.

Known for her energy, passion and "get-it-done" attitude, Jessica shares her savvy marketing tips through her weekly ezine, blog, podcasts and videos. To download your FREE Shoestring Marketing Kit, visit: www.ShoestringMarketingKit.com

TRUSTING INTUITION WHEN THE JOURNEY CHANGES

Kathleen Gage

There are days when I wonder if I am in a dream. My life is such that I deeply enjoy my business; I have a deep level of love and respect for the clients who choose me as their guide in growing their businesses; I live in a beautiful, rural community in Oregon with the love of my life and a menagerie of animals including three horses, two dogs, two cats and a goat; I enjoy a very comfortable lifestyle and have a deep belief that life is an incredible journey I have been blessed to experience.

Has it always been this way? Not at all. There was a time when my life was completely the opposite of what it is today. So what created the change? Willingness to live with a level of awareness that allows me to continually grow in spirit.

One of the most important "tools" I have used to achieve the level of appreciation I have is intuition. I have often referred to my intuition as trusting my heart.

This is an unfolding I have been experiencing for more than 30 years. I use intuition both personally and professionally.

Take my business. As far back as I can remember I have run my business on the premise of "trusting my heart" to guide me with ideas, specific actions I would benefit from taking, locations to visit that have opened up chance meetings. I also use intuition when times are uncertain. Needless to say, there would be many such times over the 17 years I have owned and operated my business.

However, there have been plenty of occasions where the head took over and always with less than optimum outcomes. It seemed the times when I chose to let my head overrule my heart, there was always a tough lesson to learn.

Actually, beginning my business was the result of following my heart. Having left a corporate job in the early nineties, I decided it was time to pursue my dream of running my own business. As if luck were on my side, within a very short time after leaving my corporate job, I secured a contract with one of the largest seminar companies in the country.

Knowing I had "arrived," I immersed myself into my newly-found fortune. I absolutely loved the travel, the ability to impact the lives of those who were in my audiences and knowing I was fulfilling a longtime dream.

After my third year on the road, I was becoming quite weary. I had stayed in more hotels, eaten in more restaurants and traveled to more cities than I could keep track of.

Although I loved being on the platform and speaking to people all around the United States and Canada, the travel and time away from home were taking their toll.

The time was fast approaching for me to let go of the contract in order to enjoy a more grounded way of life – literally and figuratively.

Although it was a somewhat tough decision due to the consistent revenue, I was very clear that the payoff was not worth it.

Taking a leap of faith, I ended the contract after a solid four-year stint. Thinking I would build my business in the local market (which was Salt Lake City at the time), within only days of making my decision, I received a call from a local career development and training company inviting me to join their executive staff. I certainly didn't expect this, but realized had I not trusted my heart and ended my contract, I might not have been in the position to so readily take the job when the offer was on the table.

The irony of this situation was I had just had a conversation with a dear friend and told her the ideal for me "right now" would be to have a job that paid well, had regular hours, no travel and was close to home. Amazingly, the new position offered all this and more.

I went from making an "OK" living to earning an excellent income that included a handsome base plus bonuses, equaling more than six figures a year. I also had the corner office, community leadership position, a great staff and incredible satisfaction with my day-to-day activities. I loved what I was doing.

Due to the nature of my job and the size of my staff, I was able to explore my creativity in marketing, sales and events development. In the first year, we increased revenues by 80 percent, substantially increased customer satisfaction and improved community awareness in leaps and bounds.

There were untold numbers of great experiences I was enjoying. I knew I had "arrived."

That is until I found out the owner was scamming investors, deceiving employees and pretty much running a number on anyone he could to the tune of $32,000,000.

The well-kept "house of cards" secret began to unravel when out of the blue some of our better vendors called and asked why they hadn't been paid in several months. I had been led to believe they were paid. When I checked with someone in the accounts payables department, I was in for quite a shock. Not only had the bills not been paid, they were stuffed in a drawer that was overflowing with unpaid invoices.

What seemed like the dream job suddenly turned into a nightmare from which I couldn't seem to awaken. The worst part was as other staff found out what was going on, they pretended like nothing was happening. I felt like I was working among a bunch of ostriches who had buried their heads in the sand.

When I confronted the owner, he simply responded, "That's the nature of business. Get used to it."

It didn't take but a moment to decide to leave. Even though the owner told me if I just looked the other way and got with the "program" I could keep getting paid, I knew in my heart of hearts I couldn't stay.

I knew in the deepest recesses of my mind and heart, even if I was not the one doing the wrong deed, to stay just to get a paycheck made me as wrong as the owner.

Although I couldn't (and wouldn't) stay with the company, I felt panic set in because I was faced with the prospect of going from a six-figure job to nothing in a matter of minutes. I also knew I was being stripped of a prestigious job to becoming someone who was suddenly unemployed. That's when the self-talk kicked in.

"You'll never find another job."

"What made you ever think you deserved a job you loved so much?"

"You may as well go to work at the local fast food!"

"You'll be the laughing-stock of this town."

I hadn't felt this alone and lost in a long time. I was angry, hurt and full of feelings of betrayal.

I really don't know how long I kept myself in this place of immobility, but one day it hit me that unless I was willing to change, nothing in the situation would change. I felt a nudging in my heart to forgive. Forgive myself, the staff and the owner. Not that I condoned what he had done, but I could forgive.

I knew I had the ability to get to the other side of this. I had been through worse situations in the past, and if this was the worst thing that could happen, it wasn't really that bad. At least not for me.

The moment I made the decision to do things differently, I felt a shift. I found myself actually grateful for the opportunity to put to the test all the things I professed to be true. For years I had studied how important our thoughts, beliefs and actions are. I also learned when one moves into gratitude, all the answers to our most challenging problems are there.

The irony about gratitude is the more we are in a state of gratitude, the more we have to be grateful for. Energetically, we attract situations that can be very joyful.

The truest sign of our sincere gratitude is when we can reside there, even when our world seems to be crumbling around us.

It was in the space of gratitude where my mind was flooding with all sorts of ideas of what I could do to right the wrongs that had been done to many of the vendors. I had a lot of guilt around what had happened. Many of the vendors who hadn't been paid in a long time were friends and colleagues who did business with the company based on my recommendation.

I decided to contact each and every person to personally apologize for what had happened to them. I recalled a very important message one of my mentors had taught me many years prior — whenever I was going to do something that involved a very emotional situation, I should ask myself what my motive was for taking the action.

I had to look in my heart to make sure I wasn't doing this for pity, ego or blame. My motives had to be completely honorable.

Amazingly, every single person said it wasn't my fault. Even though they seemed to let it go, I felt there was more I could do. I just needed to trust that whatever it was would reveal itself.

It didn't take long before it did and in the most unexpected way. Realizing I had a very strong skill at training (after all I had been on the road for four years speaking and training on the platform), I decided to invite those affected to a free seminar on customer care.

With the turn of events at the company, I had insight into what bad customer care was and was not. I was overwhelmed with gratitude at the response I received. The very people who got swindled were the very people who were more than happy to come to my seminar.

Hosting the seminar, treating everyone to an incredible day of training, and truly coming from the space of serving, things got even better than I could have imagined.

Although things were definitely on the upswing, there were also tough financial times. Going from a very comfortable income to nothing had its challenges. Trusting that "this too shall pass" was put to the test more times than I care to remember.

Yet, I was happier than I had been in some time. I knew in my heart I was doing the right thing. There are times when doing the right thing may not be very comfortable, but in the end it is worth it.

The further away I was from the painful day of leaving the job in such anger, the less I felt any pain. I had made a conscious decision not to engage in any negative talk about the situation or owner. Rather, I would focus on what I could create for my future rather than dwell on the past.

It's amazing how life will support our decisions once we do get clear on where we are going. And even though the path may not be clear and there are twists and turns along the way, when we keep the course, amazing things will transpire.

As I look back over the decade since this life-changing situation occurred, I can readily admit this was one of the most important experiences in my life.

In the 18 months I was with the company in the position of Vice President of Operations, I was able to creatively grow the company. In looking back, I realize the job security early on gave me the courage to try things in business I had not been willing to try in my own business. In my business, I had held back from my greatest potential.

When enough time passed, I realized the experience with the company was one of the greatest gifts life gave me. Not only did I grow professionally, I grew emotionally and spiritually.

I was also willing to take more risks in my own business. I made a conscious choice to pursue dreams I had been holding back on. My own business model changed in such a way that I was exploring avenues of growth into which I otherwise would never have ventured.

I have continually been given the opportunity to put trust, faith and gratitude to the test. And in the end, I am always served well as a result.

I have come to realize that my purpose in business is not to show how wonderful I am, but rather to be fully in service to my life's work. I more readily accept the unexpected twists and turns that are inevitable.

None of this would have happened had I not gone through the experience I had.

If I were to look at the many lessons I learned from this experience, I could sum it up with seven words: intuition, trust, compassion, acceptance, forgiveness, gratitude and rewards.

Intuition

Although business is very cerebral, there are plenty of times we must rely on something that has no explanation other than we have a "feeling." Some call it gut feeling, intuition, guidance or being led. What we call it does not matter as much as learning to trust it.

Some of the most incredible inventions, businesses, products and services have come out of the space of intuition. Yet, many people choose to ignore these messages.

Trust

When we are guided, this is where we must trust. This can go against everything we learned in our college business courses. Yet, it is in developing a deep level of trust that we are able to receive the blessings our business can provide us and all those who are impacted by the success of our business.

You see, the more successful a business, the more we are able to bring abundance to others. Whether it be employees, vendors, consultants or customers, trusting what we are called to do benefits everyone.

Compassion

There will be plenty of opportunity to show compassion. Not everyone will make the best choices all of the time. We are human, and we make mistakes. There are occasions we may have very poor judgment.

Acceptance

No matter how well-developed our plans, vision and expectations, there will be times when things just don't work out the way we expected. We may lose a client we expected to be with us for a long time. Somebody we thought we could trust betrays us. Perhaps an unexpected business expense shows up at the most inopportune time. Illness may strike us or a family member, and suddenly our life is upside down.

The fact is there will be plenty of unexpected circumstances in business. It's not so much what happens, it's what we do about it that makes all the difference. Do we react or do we respond? Do we resist or do we accept?

Ideally, the longer we live the easier acceptance becomes. A prayer that has been used in countless circles by millions of people is the serenity prayer.

"God grant me the serenity to accept the things I cannot change,
The courage to change the things I can,
And the wisdom to know the difference."

Acceptance doesn't make us weak. It actually empowers us. Why? Because we are in a more resourceful state of mind.

Acceptance should not be confused with passiveness. It simply means we are trusting the process of life and the path we are meant to travel.

Forgiveness

This is one of the most important lessons I have learned. When faced with disappointment, we can choose to hold on to this, or we can choose to forgive and move on. Forgiveness does not mean we agree with what has been done. It simply means we desire to live in a calmer state.

When we refuse to forgive, we allow someone to live rent-free in our minds. If we allow it, the one we hurt the most is ourselves. Lack of forgiveness can immobilize.

In order to achieve a life we love living, having the willingness to forgive is essential.

Forgiveness doesn't mean we will forget. Yet, with time, the "imprint" a tough situation may have will diminish.

Gratitude

This is one lesson I absolutely love. You could even say I am grateful for the lesson of gratitude.

When we are in the space of gratitude, magical experiences seem to appear out of nowhere. It's not so much that the experiences magically appear, it's a matter of being open and receptive to possibility.

The truest test of gratitude is to feel it, no matter what the outward circumstances. The more we express our gratitude, the more we have to be grateful for.

Some will interpret this to mean more on an outward level such as money, cars or jewels. In reality, gratitude is an inside job. And... it's contagious. Gratitude is actually great for business. It has been said, "Whatever you put out, you get in return."

Rewards

I am truly grateful for the many rewards that came from all the previous lessons I spoke of. When we follow intuition, learn to trust, practice compassion, develop a high level of acceptance, choose to forgive and express gratitude, the rewards are plentiful.

A final lesson I didn't add in the list of words is this: we never "arrive." For years I would achieve a level of success and feel like this validated my worth on some level. The truth is we never arrive. We evolve. Each experience weaves the tapestry of our lives.

Although there were plenty of times I thought I had arrived, today I am so grateful I know I will never arrive. This inspires me to evolve into my authentic self. It is a process. It is a journey. It is a blessing.

About Kathleen Gage,

Kathleen Gage, The Street Smarts Marketer™, has owned and operated her business for nearly two decades. Kathleen is recognized as a creative and effective Internet Marketing Advisor who works with spiritually minded coaches, speakers, authors and consultants who are ready to turn their knowledge into money-making information products and life-impacting services.

Kathleen is an award-winning speaker, author and entrepreneur. She has been a featured speaker at conferences and conventions. She is the host of Daily Awareness radio show and has been a featured guest on hundreds of teleseminars and radio programs. Her signature series, Street Smarts Marketing and Promotions, is a favorite of thousands of clients around the globe. Kathleen's greatest passion is working with those who realize and accept their role in raising the consciousness of business. Visit her online at www.KathleenGage.com.

HUMAN BEING OR HUMAN DOING?

Dr. Linda Miles

"The key is not to prioritize what's on your schedule, but to schedule your priorities."
—Stephen Covey

It all started the day I went to a training session on a busy Friday morning. As I entered the classroom, I stumbled because I was preoccupied with reading my daily "to do" list. Working as director of crisis programs for a large mental health center, I was slammed with administrative assignments. I had no idea that the class was about to spark a transformation in my life.

Entering the room that day, I had yet to realize that I had become a "human doing" instead of a human being. Unconsciously, I was acting out scripts programmed in my brain by family, culture, the media, magazines, influential others, and whatever else. Like most people, I had made important unconscious decisions about what my life should look like by the time I walked through the door of elementary school.

HUMAN DOING

My heart was all about being a psychotherapist, yet I had allowed my ego to take over my career. My ego loved the thrill of promotions and being "in charge." I lost my awareness of and gratitude for the present moment. I was preoccupied by the past or the future as I stumbled into class that Friday over thirty years ago.

What was my head telling me?

1. Go for security!
2. You have to please others!
3. Do the things that impress others.

What was my heart telling me?

1. Follow your heart!
2. You have a purpose that others do not comprehend!
3. Follow your bliss. Do the work that your hand goes to naturally.

There is a saying that when the student is ready, the teacher will appear. The class was called "Introduction to Time Management." My "human doing" self had chosen the class to become more efficient, but it was a transformation of my soul that began that morning. My Higher Self was ignited as I considered this class assignment:

CLASS ASSIGNMENT

Write a description of how you want your life to be in 5 years, including a paragraph on work, love, and play. What would your ideal job look like? How would the day go? How much would you make? What would your love life look like? Describe your ideal family life. In your ideal world, what do you do for relaxation and recreation? Choose a partner in the class and share what you have written. Make an agreement to meet in one year and discuss the progress you have made.

MY HEART

My heart pounced on this exercise. When I partnered with a colleague to discuss the assignment, I shared my heart's vision for marriage, family life, work, and recreation. I had an amazing clarity about my ideal life. There was something magical about writing down my heart's desires.

INTERNAL LOCUS OF CONTROL

This was the beginning of an internal locus of control in my life. I took the first steps toward transformation and living my dreams of working in a successful private practice as a psychotherapist, writing books and articles, living with my perfect marriage partner, and balancing love, work, and play.

INTENTION

This class introduced me to the notion of intention. Intention is focusing on the present moment, bringing inner strength to goals over time. As I considered the difference between the life I was living and the life I wanted, I realized that I was choosing the wrong road in every area of my life. This class was a catalyst to help me shine a light on my unconscious intentions. As Yongey Mingyur Rinpoche observed, "Ultimately happiness comes down to choosing between the discomfort of becoming aware of your mental afflictions and the discomfort of being ruled by them." That morning I became aware of the negative messages that were running my life. I had been inhibited by a sense of inadequacy and fear of rejection that held me back from being authentic and alive in the moment. Dr. Seuss may have had this self-consciousness in mind when he urged us to jettison inhibitions and heed the call of life:

"Let us quit all this waiting and staying and go to the place where the boom band is playing."

How did I move in the direction of my dreams after I became aware of my negative mental patterns and clarified my positive intentions? First, I had to train my brain to let go of ego speak and embrace a higher reality of the Spirit.

In learning to live from my heart, an essential lesson was that my UNCONSCIOUS was running the show. I often see clients who think that they should be able to make great decisions consciously and who are down on themselves because they make some dumb choices. Once they understand that the unconscious is in charge and go to the root of their fears, they make progress.

HEARTSMART

Thirty years ago, when I began to pay attention to my heart, neuroscience had yet to unlock many secrets of the brain that have affirmed and informed my practice. Some of these discoveries of neuroscience include:

1. The structure of the brain changes with negative experiences, especially those that happen when we are children.
2. We can train our brains to move in more positive directions and rewire more positive thoughts and perceptions.
3. With some insight and self-awareness, you can develop a short list of decisions that interfere with your optimal functioning (e.g., my belief that I HAD to please others or ELSE) and recognize the roots of recurring upsets.
4. Once you recognize the roots of recurring upsets, you can convert suffering into creative problem solving.

5. Through practice, you can learn to live in an openhearted way and embrace the joy of the present moment.

EGO-SPEAK

As I thought about the questions in the simple exercise, I was shocked by how far I had wandered from my heart and purpose in life. After I wrote my answers to the questions in the exercise, I sat down with a colleague, Dr. Jim Alfred, to discuss the implications. Dr. Alfred was old enough to be my father, a wise and loving psychiatrist and father of five. I blurted out that I wished to leave my position as administrator and become a psychotherapist, but was torn because doing so would let people down. He smiled and asked, "Has it ever occurred to you that you might have a job that helps others and also honors you?" He nailed it—I was so busy trying to please and impress others that I lost myself.

In *Mere Christianity,* C.S. Lewis observed that the principles Jesus taught have practical applications, because when we follow the directions, our lives work. When we follow cultural or childhood programming to pursue power and money, we're almost always let down. A plaque on our wall reads, "There is only one happiness—to love and be loved" (George Sand). It reminds me of what is important. My transformation began with the examination of the UNCONSCIOUS messages that were taking me away from my own heart and purpose.

The wise spiritual advice to "Love one another as thyself" requires a balance between self and others. I realized that I loved others INSTEAD of myself. I had gotten lost trying to impress others and paid no attention to my own heart's desires and purpose. I was taking care of my ego self and ignoring my heart and Higher Self.

BEGIN AT THE END

I began a journey toward my dreams on that Friday morning by setting goals with my heart. Over the years, there were many times when my heart was challenged, and I thought it might be easier to return to living in my head. In those dark times I would always return to choosing love as my motivation — a balance of love between self and others was my inner guide. I encourage clients to begin at the end, set goals, and then be prepared to meet inevitable challenges. Following your heart is a KNOWING, and following your fears is a REACTION. Most fears are based on the past and we need to challenge these notions.

LIVING LIFE BY CHOICE

Although we can never be conscious of all that is in our hearts and minds, learning to live my life by choice guided my actions in the years after I woke up in the workshop. Of course, this was a process over time, but I would like to share some of the practices that transformed my life and greatly expanded my income. Bottom line, it was about clear intention to:

- Express deep, authentic self.
- Develop spiritual practices to transcend ego.
- Find a calm and peaceful place within.
- Celebrate every day.
- Spark inner happiness.
- Take time out to center before saying or doing destructive things.
- Live in the moment.
- Choose peace of mind instead of attack thoughts.
- Develop constructive and creative outlets.
- Accept what is.

- Stop blaming and start living.
- Refrain from damaging dramas.
- Seek inspiration, wisdom, and positive role models.
- Unite the fire of heart with the sacred path that connects you to a higher reality of the spirit.
- Allow negative feelings to flow through without becoming attached.
- Deal with grief.
- Invite the presence of God.

DREAMS ARE IN YOUR NEIGHBORHOOD

After the workshop, I began a steady practice of affirmations to program my brain to look for my deepest intentions. I began to consciously choose love instead of fear as my motivation. With great angst, I resigned my administrative position, began working part-time as a psychotherapist, and headed back to Florida State University for a doctorate. I learned that when I am on my true path, things fall into place.

As I retrained my brain to look for my deepest intentions, I realized they were already in my neighborhood, but I had missed them because our brains only sees what we expect to see. I had tripped over opportunities to live more authentically when my ego ran the show. My perfect job as a psychotherapist was right around the corner from my former administrative office, my ideal partner and future husband had been a friend and colleague for eight years, and I already lived in a beautiful section of North Florida. I start each day with the affirmation, "I thank God for joy and love and miracles" to draw my attention to the abundance all around me.

Inuit families in extremely cold climates see over one hundred kinds of snow because their brains has been trained to recognize the difference. As I programmed my brain to search out my heart's desires, I found the ideal work, love, and play that I pictured and achieved financial abundance. As I crowded out negative thoughts and intentions with positive pictures, I began rewiring my brain with positive pathways. Neuroscientist Dr. Wayne Drevets writes, "In the brain practice makes permanent."

CLEAR INTENTION

As you focus your mind with clear intention, your unconscious mind moves in the direction of your goal. Have you ever had the experience of wanting a certain kind of car and then seeing ones like it everywhere? This is because your conscious mind can only focus on seven things, while your unconscious has unlimited capacity. Right now, your unconscious is operating your entire body — so if you turn your attention to how you are sitting, you will realize that you unconsciously moved your muscles and positioned yourself. Statements of intention help you program your brain in the direction of your dreams.

SELF-PROGRAM YOUR BRAIN WITH WHAT IS MOST IMPORTANT

As I write this, we are looking forward to the birth of a new grandson in a month. I see pregnant women, babies, and little boys everywhere I go these days. The spotlight in my brain shines on diapers and baby products in the grocery since my unconscious is primed to notice such things; last year, I could have tripped over baby stuff and not noticed. Although I have ignored the baby aisle for years, my spotlight is focused on baby items because my grandson's upcoming birth is important to me. Self-program your brain with what is most important to you. In your heart, you know the secrets to your happiness. Let your statements and intention remind you of who you truly are.

Your brain follows the pictures in your mind's eye. The right occupation or partner could be under your nose, and you might not notice that this is the perfect person for you, because you are not clear about what you want. Clarity of thought is needed when you seek to follow your heart.

PICTURE YOUR PERFECT FLOWER

Don't be like a butterfly flitting from flower to flower to find what you want by trial and error. Picture your perfect flower and let it grow in the quiet of your mind.

YOUR TURN

"We have what we seek, it is there all the time, and if we give it time, it will make itself known to us" (Thomas Merton).

When you are aware of how you have been programmed by the past, you are free to reprogram your dreams. Picture what you want based on love for yourself and others, and then say, write, or even sing what you want often. In the brain, *practice makes permanent*. Make your statements and intentions reflect personal and spiritual values.

I thank God for my ideal relationship.
I thank God for inner peace.
I thank God for my life of joy, love, and miracles.

You need to repeat statements of intention as often as possible. Say them, sing them, write them, and live them! Track intentions and meaningful questions in a daily journal.

These statements help reprogram your brain and invite the help of your higher self through your unconscious.

JOURNALS

Over the years I kept a journal, and now I have a record of how I have lived toward my dreams by manifesting a successful private psychotherapy practice; an award winning book, *The New Marriage*; numerous articles for national magazines; CDs; bookings on national television and radio; and a new book, *Friendship on Fire*, a guide for couples. I spelled out specifics of my dreams in the journal and checked them off when they came true.

Keeping a journal is an integral tool to do the following:

- Blow off steam.
- Look at patterns over time.
- Get to know yourself.
- Write down life lessons.
- Write statements of intention.
- Keep inspirational phrases.
- Keep track of progress.
- Look at a situation from a different perspective.
- Take time out to calm down.

KEEPING A JOURNAL

Keeping a journal or diary for five years is an amazing, yet simple tool that supports and enhances you. With your journal, you learn and empower your positive intentions. Within the pages of your journal, you will begin to observe and recognize what you want to do differently, because it no longer works for you.

When you write your thoughts and experiences in a journal, you can actually see what you are thinking because you are putting your thoughts into a solid, tangible form. Patterns of thinking and doing, which we all have, are easily observed when recorded on paper. Creating a written record over five years helps to track and record daily life: where you are, where you were, and especially where we want to go. Journals are a proven, effective method for personal growth that helps us focus, clarify, and reduce stress.

Using an already formatted book like *The 5 Year Journal* (www.the5yearjournal.com) is an easy way to keep your relationship journal. You can also use a computer or a blank book or notebook with enough pages to record three lines per day for five years.

Every day, on one line, succinctly journal your summarized answer to each of the three following questions:

1. What is most important to you about today?
2. What lesson did you learn today?
3. What affirmation or goal do you have for one year from today?

Examples:

1. *Today I saw myself changing for the better.*
2. *I learned the difference between needs and needy.*
3. *I thank God for my perfect physical, mental, emotional, spiritual, and financial health.*

JOURNALING TIPS

You may start your journal on any day of the year. Set your journal where you will see it every day: on the kitchen table, your desk, or in your briefcase. This will help remind you to journal daily.

Keep a pen or pencil with your journal. Skipping days is a part of journaling. You can use the same color of pen or use different colors. You can also designate colors of pens for certain feelings (e.g., green = growth, blue =sadness, orange = joy, red = anger). If you are using different-colored pens, write in the front of your journal what each color signifies. Journals are an easy, fun, and interesting way to discover more about ourselves and each other.

Some other questions to answer in your journal:

Where were you a year ago?
What were you doing 2 years ago?
What were you feeling 3 years ago?
What were your dreams 5 years ago?

Journal daily the next 5 years in minutes a day!

REVIEW

To summarize the activities that have helped me and countless others follow our hearts, live consciously, and create abundance:

1. Awareness of negative thought patterns and how they run your life
2. Creation of positive intentions
3. Making time every day for practice and evaluation of intentions

Think of the acronym "AIM" to remember the steps toward transformation of your life:

A = Awareness
I = Intention
M = Making time for practice and evaluation

Before my teacher arrived in the form of a time management class, I was unaware of the unconscious programming that ran my life. Step one of change is awareness so you can begin to live your life by choice.

Intention is vital as you change patterns in your brain. Because our brains love the familiar, we are drawn repeatedly to patterns that may be destructive. There were many obstacles in my path when I lived from my ego, pleased others, and chose security at any cost. Joseph Campbell wrote that when you come to the end of a path, you need to JUMP. I had to JUMP on many occasions!

I recommend to clients that having a safety net for potential consequences, but there are many times when you have to follow your heart with clear intention. There were many times when I was discouraged, but I kept up my practice of intention and did not become cynical. I KNEW in my heart that I needed to live from my Higher Self.

GET OUT THERE

Once you set clear intentions, you have to get out there and market. Some of the best strategies I've tried:

1. Gather a team. You can do this at low or no cost by asking friends to evaluate your work, finding interns from local universities, or using social networking.

2. Offer to speak about your niche to local groups and media.
3. Be nice (this was great advice from my mother) — to build alliances.
4. Network. Find kindred spirits. This book is an example, as I have an on-going collaboration with Marnie at IdeaMarketers. (She is top drawer.)
5. Find role models. Watch Katie Couric or Diane Sawyer and ask yourself: What are they doing to communicate effectively?
6. Listen to feedback even if it hurts — in fact the best feedback probably will sting.
7. If you hear from a big producer, let him or her LEAD. (I made the mistake of telling a producer all my opinions instead of listening to what SHE wanted and lost out on the opportunity.)

The Principles of AIM Practice are:

1. *Stop the worthless dance:* Notice the ways that you replay past programming and work on healing the self-lie that you are worthless. When these negative thoughts arise in your mind, imagine that the thought is surrounded by a transparent bubble and that you can send the bubble off to God for healing.
2. *Do not despise. Visualize:* Avoid envy of others and transform that energy into positive intentions. If you find that you are jealous of something in someone else, ask yourself what that jealous reaction signals that you want to manifest in your own life. For example, if a friend is successful in writing a book and you feel jealous, it could be that you also want to write.
3. *Practice the Present:* Ask yourself, "What is real in the present moment?" and notice when you are living in your head. Embrace the miracles around you through your senses.

As Rainer Maria Rilke wrote, we need to learn to love the questions in life, and we must live our way to the answers. Changing our unconscious programs and living positive intentions requires practice. Choose love instead of fear to guide your process. Trust your heart to give you a map and take the journey. You can transform your ideas into income because, if you live your true purpose, there are those who need what you have to offer.

In summary:

1. Begin with the ending.
2. Choose love instead of fear as your motivation.
3. Trust your heart to KNOW your true purpose.
4. Learn lessons from inevitable wrong turns.
5. Learn from your REACTIONS: Look for the root of unconscious fears in your past.
6. Live with love and Intention instead of fear and reaction.
7. Look for role models.
8. Listen to your higher self for direction.
9. Stop blaming and start living.
10. Embrace the joy, love, and miracles that surround you.

Dr. Linda Miles
Dr. Miles has worked in the field of mental health for over thirty years as a psychotherapist, consultant, educator and writer. She has appeared on national television and radio programs as well as in magazines such as *Woman's World*, *Parents* and *Entrepreneur*. She wrote the award-winning book "*The New Marriage, Transcending the Happily Ever After Myth*" with her husband (Dr. Robert Miles). She has recently published "*All Aboard The Brain Train: Teaching Your Child to Live With Purpose,*" a book about relationships written for children, "*Amanda Salamander Discovers the Secret to Happily Ever After.*" Her latest book "*Friendship on Fire*" is a practical guide to relationships.

Dr. Linda Miles

Dr. Miles has won numerous professional awards such as "Outstanding Educator in Business and Industry," from Florida State University and "Outstanding Contributions to Knowledge in the Practice of Marriage and Family Therapy" by TAMFT.

She serves in the National Advisory Board of Access Technologies Social Simentor Model for Intervention with Autism and was recently appointed by the President of the Florida Senate to The Florida Commission on Support Initiatives for Marriage and Family.

She is listed in *Who's Who Among American Women*, (Marquis,1993). Dr. Miles has a passion for helping create a better world through loving relationships. Visit her online at www.DrLindaMiles.com

REINVENTING YOURSELF

Milana Leshinsky

They say that if it ain't broke, don't fix it. In business, however, that's not always true.

I had been making good money for several years working with life coaches. But I knew that if a business wasn't growing, it would soon start shrinking. So I made a decision to shift my focus to a new market in the hope of expanding my business and my reach.

This is a scary thing to do, especially if your "old" market has been your bread and butter and the primary source of income for your entire family.

Helping life coaches build businesses online was my exclusive focus. As my business matured, I realized that my most successful clients – those who were making six figures and enjoying their lifestyle – created multiple streams of income in their businesses. The light bulb came on, and I saw this as a great business model I could easily teach to other service professionals. This would not only help me greatly expand my reach, but would also allow me to have a bigger impact in the world and grow my income.

So I went from working with coaches to helping service-based business owners create multiple income streams businesses.

There were quite a few challenges in making this transition.

At the beginning, I really felt like my idea was too easy of a solution, too obvious of a project, too simple as my next step in business. I felt like I needed to do more research, brainstorming, asking around, and consulting my mentors instead of simply jumping in and doing it.

In addition, the newly-proposed model went completely against my own teachings. I believe in focusing on a specific niche market and building "deep" by developing a line of products, programs, and services to support the market. The "service industry" is too broad to be a niche market, so I knew I needed a different approach. I couldn't just implement the same marketing strategy that I used to succeed in my coaching market.

After serving life coaches for nearly ten years, I really knew my market and my topic. I was part of this group of people, so I had a lot of challenges, goals, and dreams in common with them. I had conducted dozens of surveys, live events, coaching, and private conversations with these people. I could close my eyes and tell you what they desired the most. I think that knowing what drives your target market to do what they do every day helps you make profitable decisions.

"Service-based business owners" was a new market for me. Life coaches are certainly service professionals, but most of them work from home without any employees. Branching out into other service-based industries made me think of people like my financial advisor, accountant, chiropractor, massage therapist, and dentist. Now I was talking to someone who probably had a physical location and staff. They saw clients or patients all day long, and their minds were occupied with different issues.

In addition to creating more income and getting more clients, they were also thinking about keeping their waiting rooms clean, their receptionists professional, and their schedules manageable. They had to worry about their rent, utilities, supplies, and payroll.

Without fully understanding the market or doing extensive research, I felt hesitant. Most of all, I really craved feedback from an experienced business mentor who could tell me if this was the right strategic decision.

But after a few months of thinking about it, I realized that I so truly believed in the benefits of turning a service-based business into a multiple-income-streams business that I decided to move forward with this idea despite all my doubts.

I've seen so many people turn their businesses – and lives – around after they discovered this new model! Service business owners will NEVER get rich unless they shift into a multiple income streams business model. I knew I could easily teach it to the frustrated and burned-out service professionals who wanted to grow their businesses but had no more "bandwidth."

I became so excited about the new direction, I couldn't wait to get started! I could already see myself implementing the new business model and enjoying the results. I could see myself on stage presenting my new program and people in the audience filling out their applications to enroll.

I noticed that when I get excited and passionate about an idea, it's almost always a success. And not for any logical or research-based reason, but because my passion moves it forward.

I became completely unstoppable and frankly didn't care what anyone said to me at that point. I've had times when people didn't believe in my new ideas (or me), but I went for them anyway. I knew that if I only stuck to it and saw my idea through, I would succeed.

My mind was exploding with possibilities of a new marketing and business growth strategy. Normally I would create a system, a curriculum, or a program for my niche market, and launch it to my mailing list with the help of my joint venture partners. I needed something different here, because I no longer was industry-specific. I tried to remember how other companies I wanted to model looked - like E-Myth, Strategic Coach, Sandler Training - even people like Oprah. I felt like I needed to think bigger, bolder, and get more serious about growing my business if I wanted to go beyond seven figures.

Getting started was tough. My idea was exciting, but so big, I felt like I needed to sit down and plan it all on paper. Then I'd run it by my best friend, who'd most likely support me just because she'd see my excitement and believe in me.

First, I scheduled time with myself, then with my friend, and finally I turned to my mastermind group. Once everything was clear in my mind, I created a timeline for the next 12 months to implement my ideas.

One of the biggest obstacles I saw ahead of me was trying to clearly explain the concept of multiple income streams to service business owners, who traditionally focused on getting clients and filling their practices. I started questioning whether my idea was worth pursuing, because I knew my market needed to be educated before they'd buy. After all, it's always easier to sell to someone who's already aware of the problem in their current situation.

I knew that the only way service professionals would invest with me was if they understood that they couldn't grow their traditional service business or private practice further, unless they were willing to add more clients or more staff. They had to be in a place where they WANTED to change things in their lives.

I decided to continue serving coaches, while gradually making the move on the new expanded market I chose. That way I could keep my "bread and butter" market and confidently move forward into the new ones.

I also had to be okay with not being able to get through to everyone. When the student is ready, the teacher will appear. I would much rather help those who are ready for my help than those who need to be convinced. It took my best friend two years of being around me to go from being a professional organizer to becoming an information marketer. She can now work from home and stay with her little boy, while just a few years ago it seemed like an impossible dream. When I asked what caused her to finally make the decision to change to a new business, she answered, "I was just ready."

So I asked myself, "How can I get people ready?" The most brilliant solution came to mind! I decided that writing a book could kill many birds with one stone. My new book *Dough for What You Know* would become a perfect tool for me to explain why a traditional service-based business was difficult to grow. Then I would introduce the new model of multiple income streams business, which businesses could use to grow without adding more clients or hiring more people. The book would help me introduce and clarify the concept and move prospects to invest in my Multiple Income Streams program.

A book is always a great marketing tool! It's very non-threatening to offer someone a book instead of asking them to hire you right away. The book educates, creates mind shifts, and gets people ready to say yes or no. Some people would likely read it and say, "I am fine where I am today," and that's okay. But those people who'd been looking for an easier way to grow their service business would realize, "Wow! This is exactly what I need!" Then they might move forward with me.

As I was writing the book, I was also learning to clearly communicate my ideas to the new market. It's like developing a muscle - you have to keep talking about it, writing about it, and helping people with it before you really become knowledgeable and confident about your topic.

In the end, I had to see myself giving a copy of my book to my financial advisor, chiropractor, dentist, massage therapist, or my daughter's piano teacher, and feel confident that they would GET it. They might not be ready to work with me or move forward with the multiple-income-streams business model yet, but I wanted them to see this as an amazing opportunity to grow.

What have I learned in the process of making the transition? Here are my most important lessons, which I hope will help you make your business growth easier and more enjoyable.

Lesson #1: Creating a profitable business is 20% about products and 80% about marketing.

I knew I could've easily started creating products for my new market, but I didn't want to end up with products that nobody wanted. I see a lot of people spend so much time on creating and polishing up their products and programs, but when the time comes to generate income from them, they get stuck.

Everything in business is about marketing. Take a mediocre product and market the heck out of it, and you'll be much better off than with an excellent product and mediocre marketing. Show me a best-selling product, and I'll show you a brilliant marketer behind it, who came up with a great strategy to attract massive attention to the product.

Marketing is not just about the strategy. It's also about visibility. The more people see you or hear about you, the more they perceive you as the ultimate expert in your field. In fact, I have a poster over my computer that says, "Always Be Visible!" You might have times when you don't have any promotions or new products, so you might decide that you can take a break from marketing or sending your newsletter out. Try disappearing for a couple of months, and people will think you went out of business.

Many entrepreneurs struggle because they don't market their businesses consistently. I truly believe that if you focus on becoming marketing-savvy for the next six months, your business will grow like never before.

Lesson #2: There are a million ways to make a million dollars. You just have to find the right way for you.

Too many people decide to do something just because it worked for someone else. One of my old mentors wanted me to travel around the country attending networking meetings a couple of times a month, so I could meet and connect with potential customers. As much as I wanted to grow my business, I was stuck for a year feeling completely paralyzed – simply because this was the wrong approach for me.

I remember starting a coaching club years ago, in which I had to hold group coaching calls twice a month and offer support on a membership forum. My goal was to enroll 200 members. After about four months, I couldn't stand running it! The most members I ever attracted was 24 people, and a year later I shut it down.

A colleague of mine, who started her coaching club at about the same time, grew it to 125 members, and continues to run it years later. Was she a better marketer? Did her club offer more value? Not at all. I simply dreaded the format and subconsciously resisted growing it further.

There is no right or wrong business model, just like there is no right or wrong marketing strategy. There is only the right one for you. I call it a "gut check." If it doesn't feel right in my body, I abandon the idea. If you're not passionate about an idea, then no matter how great it worked for someone else, you will be struggling with it. On the other hand, if a particular model hasn't worked for someone you know, or if people tell you it's not going to work, but you feel the "fire in your belly," then go for it! Your passion and belief will drive it forward.

Lesson #3: Everyone buys differently. Your product mix must accommodate all buyers.

There are 3 kinds of buyers in the world. Those who want to do everything themselves ("Do-It-Yourself") will usually choose to pay the lowest prices you offer. Those who want hand-holding ("Help-Me-Do-It") are willing to pay more to get feedback and support along the way. This is where coaching fits in. And those who want someone else to do it for them ("Done-For-You") are willing to pay whatever you charge as long as they don't have to touch it!

When you create a multiple-income-streams business, your goal is to cater to all three kinds of buyers and budgets. Not only will you attract more customers this way, but you will also keep more customers.

Imagine a customer who buys your book. She's really excited about it and after reading it, she is ready to dive in and implement. But there is no next step – no support, no coaching, and no one to ask questions. Just the book. What does she do? She goes online and finds someone else to help her. You lose a customer and leave thousands of dollars on the table.

Now imagine a different scenario. You offer consulting, and your average package is $2500. A prospect comes to you and wants to work with you, but can't afford your services. So she asks you if she can get your help in a less expensive arrangement. Unless you have a group workshop or a home-study course, she'll be walking away without giving you a penny, and most likely turning to another expert for help. Moreover, when she finds what suits her budget, she may upgrade to a more expensive package later – but it will not be with you!

So, you see, it's essential to have offerings at different pricing levels and in different formats. That's how you create a lifetime customer!

Lesson #4: Know exactly whom you serve and what problem you solve.

Bill Cosby said, "I don't know the key to success, but the key to failure is trying to please everybody." I've seen hundreds of entrepreneurs who struggle because they can't make a decision about their niche. After ten years of running her business, a woman was still struggling to make $30,000 a year. At the same time, I knew nothing about running a business, but earned $106,000 in my third year simply because I made a fast niche decision.

Many books have been written about choosing the right niche, and many programs have been created to help entrepreneurs in this process. So all I am going to say is that the best niche markets consist of people who can be easily found in large groups. They share similar challenges and get together to find solutions. If you can't easily reach your target audience, you'd better have a huge marketing budget to find them one by one.

Lesson #5: People don't want a comprehensive system. They want small steps to get quick wins and move on.

When I first started my business, I tried to stuff as much value as possible into my products. So I always ended up with hundreds of pages, hours of videos and audios, and lists of resources for people. That's because when I thought of "value," I thought of "content."

As the Internet evolved and all kinds of information became freely available, people have never felt more overwhelmed and overloaded than today. Unless your information is extremely unique and specialized, most people will not value "more information." Instead, they'll put a lot higher value on a well-filtered and well-organized system that gives them just what they need to succeed.

This is great news for information product developers! Instead of slaving for months or years to create a home-study course or a comprehensive all-inclusive program, we can create short lessons or nuggets of information and focus on implementation. Give people worksheets, exercises, access to support, live Q&A calls, and other ways to take quick action and see results.

People are more likely to invest into home-study courses if they made a decision to master a skill or become an expert on a particular topic. But more often than not, they will go for a less information-intensive option.

My top 3 favorite types of products include micro-membership programs (courses delivered one segment at a time, which will also generate monthly recurring revenue for you!), small laser-focused products (each one addressing a specific challenge, tactic, or strategy), and coaching (implementation support with access to you).

I never considered myself to be a risk-taker. But when I look over the last ten years of my life, I realize that I probably am. Not the kind who plunges from a plane, or the kind who invests 90% of her savings into a potentially profitable venture. But starting a new business, holding your first live event, partnering with people you never met, and going after a new market are ALL decisions of a risk-taker.

Or perhaps these are decisions made from trusting your heart. At least, that's always been true for me. Every day I do a "gut check" and ask, "Does it feel right? Am I still excited? Do I feel good about my decision?"

I also ask myself this important question. "Based on my past experiences, is this going to work?" Trust your heart, but always check in with your mind. If both give you a "go-ahead," then move forward with your ideas, and don't let anyone burst your bubble!

About Milana Leshinsky
Milana had a zero chance of success. She came from a country where business didn't exist, some of the most brilliant people lived in poverty, and the world's best books could only be bought on the "black market." In just a few short years — after looking for ways to stay home

with her two small children—she figured out how to create simple, money-making information products and turned her favorite topics into a million-dollar business from home. Starting her business with just a hundred dollars in the bank, Milana is now considered one of the top experts in her field. Through her programs and events Milana has trained thousands of aspiring entrepreneurs on how to turn their passion into cash. Visit her online at http://www.Milana.com.

FROM ER TO ENTREPRENEUR

Ellen Britt

Like many people who own and run an online business, I didn't start out making my living as I do today. I came to my current situation from a world very far removed from marketing...the world of a busy Emergency Room.

I grew up in a small business environment, so you might think entrepreneurship would have come naturally to me. But that's not quite the way things worked out.

You see, my parents owned and operated a commercial greenhouse, and even though they relished "being their own bosses," I saw (and experienced myself) just how hard they worked for every single dollar they earned…

… getting up every day before dawn to go out to the greenhouses to plant hundreds of boxes of seeds, working endless hours transplanting delicate young plants, shoveling and mixing truckloads of potting soil, watering thirsty azaleas under the hot Southern sun...

…and yes, waiting on customers, who kept coming back year after year for their beautiful flowers and exceptional customer service.

My parents used some of their hard-earned money to send me to college and then to PA school. After graduation, anxious to try my wings, I moved to upstate New York and began my career in medicine.

For more than two decades, I worked as a physician assistant or PA in urgent care clinics and hospital emergency rooms, treating people who came through the doors with everything from chainsaw lacerations and broken bones to pneumonia and even heart attacks.

Pretty exciting work by anyone's standards! But I was completely and utterly miserable. Now please don't misunderstand. I adored my patients, and I loved my actual work. And I was very good at what I did.

But I absolutely hated being boxed in by a demanding schedule of long, grueling hours, having to work nights and nearly every holiday, and most of all, I deeply resented being dependent on someone else to tell me what they thought I was worth.

I longed for a way out. So I went back to school and got a Masters and then a doctorate in biology. Well, let me tell you, those degrees didn't help me elevate my earning power one bit. I was forced back into working again as a PA so I could support myself and my family.

Soon I found myself mired in misery again. Not knowing what else to do and being pretty good at the student thing, I tried the "go back to school" solution once again. While still employed full-time as a PA, I entered a distance learning doctoral program in psychology, and after years of working nights and weekends towards yet another degree (and going deeper and deeper into debt), I finally had to abandon my plans.

I did escape with a Masters in psychology, but once again, another degree did nothing to propel me to monetary success. In fact, I was in worse financial shape than ever.

When I tried to talk about my distress with my friends and PA colleagues, they didn't want to hear it. "Ellen," they would respond, shaking their heads in disbelief, "you are an experienced PA with a specialty in Emergency Medicine. You're also at the top of your salary scale, with a great job and good benefits. Why would you want to give all this up? There are lots of people who would just love to be in your shoes!"

When I thought logically about it, I really couldn't argue with them. I had spent many years getting my medical education and was not likely to find another job that would pay as much or I would like any better. I quit talking about my misery and just resigned myself to try as hard as I could to cultivate a better attitude.

But my heart wouldn't quit asking me questions…questions that seemed to pop into my head the moment I let my guard down. This "heart-voice" as I came to refer to it, kept whispering, "What if there really was a way out, Ellen? What would that look like?"

I thought about those questions every single day, but no satisfactory answers seemed to be forthcoming.

Then late one night, I had a dream. Not just any dream, mind you, but a dream so vivid and so real, it was more like a vision. In the dream I was walking in the middle of a walled medieval courtyard.

All around me were beautiful young maidens, dressed in flowing garments and dancing around a Maypole.

Out of the corner of one eye, I sensed a slight movement near a half-open gate in the courtyard's stone wall. A radiant woman approached me, dressed in a nun's habit of pure white and robin's egg blue. As we came face-to-face, her eyes, which were a startling azure, looked deeply into mine. Then, to my complete surprise, she placed her palm gently on my lower abdomen and said softly, "I'm so glad about the coming child!" At once, I realized I was pregnant, and simultaneously I awakened and sat bolt upright in bed.

For weeks, the dream remained vividly real in my mind's eye. I didn't even have to ask myself what this could mean. I was convinced that I was meant to have a child.

At age forty-four, pregnancy was not an option. Then one day, a few weeks after the dream, I was flooded with the certainty that I should adopt, and I immediately began research on how best to approach this.

My heart-voice, usually so persistent on the matter of my medical career, was strangely silent on the matter. No further questions bubbled into my head. Perhaps, I thought, this is what I am meant to do.

Eighteen months later, after completing reams of paperwork, undergoing countless interviews, being fingerprinted multiple times and enduring a seventeen-hour flight to mainland China, an exquisite infant girl with liquid dark eyes was placed in my arms. My dream was fulfilled, and I was suffused with a sense of contentment. Perhaps the angst I had constantly felt over my job had been banished forever.

After my "maternity" leave, I returned to work, and for a time, the heart-voice remained silent. I settled into the routine of work and childcare, with the occasional airplane flight back to my native Georgia to visit my parents with the baby. But each time I visited, I found it more and more difficult to leave. My parents were aging, and they were the only grandparents my child would ever know.

Soon, the heart-voice began speaking to me again. But this time, the questions were not about career, but about the intense longing I felt to be near my parents and to return to my native Georgia. Once again, I battled with my logical side, the part of me that said I couldn't possibly give up my job and move, especially now that I had a child and all the responsibilities that come with parenthood.

But God had other plans. My future came to me, this time not in the form of a dream, but with the stark reality of a phone call telling me that my beloved elderly dad had broken his hip and was on the way to the hospital.

Within six months of that phone call, I had found a less than ideal PA job in a clinic a half-hour away from my parents' house and relocated to Georgia. My heart's calling seemed to be satisfied, and I heard no more from the interior voice.

But later that same year, distress over my job came creeping in again. I tried rather unsuccessfully to make the best of it. My heart-voice was silent.

Then one day, my physician supervisor asked me to do something I believed was frankly unethical. At that moment, the heart-voice spoke, and rather loudly this time, saying, "Ellen, this is the door."

So I walked away, leaving a two-decade long career in medicine and the certainly of a regular paycheck behind me.

Today, I own a successful online marketing consulting and coaching business. My schedule, my time and my ultimate worth are what I decide they should be. And yes, the early years after I left medicine were anything but easy.

But I learned some important lessons in those years, lessons I could have never gained from any amount of formal education. Here are nine of the most valuable lessons I learned from following my heart, along with a question for you to think about after each lesson:

Lesson One: Qualities developed in one area can be carried over to another.

For quite some time after I left my PA job, even though I knew I never wanted to return to medicine, I felt inadequate and unprepared as a marketer. But then, I began to discover I could transfer the same qualities that had made me an excellent PA to my new profession.

For example, I learned that successful entrepreneurs were decisive. They took in pertinent information and then made their decision. No waffling or wasting time.

I had spent years making hundreds of quick decisions during every 12-hour shift I worked; from what questions to ask my patients to which diagnostic tests to order, to what medicines to prescribe for their treatment. This was an area in which I excelled.

Question One: What qualities do you possess that have been honed by past experience and that you can bring to your current business or the business you want to start?

Lesson Two: Knowledge and experience are enduring and can be applied to any area of work and life.

I find that many things learned in my medical career actually give me a distinct advantage over many other marketing coaches and consultants who do not (and cannot) have the same combination of education and experience.

In my two decades plus as a PA, I treated over 100,000 patients. As a result, I have honed my interviewing skills to a fine edge. This has served me well in my new business.

Over the last few years, I have put these skills to good use by hosting eight telesummits, and I have interviewed some of the biggest and most well-known names in internet marketing as well as self-development: Dr. Joe Vitale, Mark Joyner, Marcie Shimoff, Peggy McColl, Dr. Jean Houston, Dave Lakhani, Janet Attwood, Lynne McTaggart, Ryan Lee, Chunyi Lin, Dr. Al Sears, Willie Crawford, Tellman Knudson and many others. Nearly every single person I have interviewed has told me I am the best interviewer they have ever experienced.

During my time at PA school, I was also taught a highly specialized, systematic way of approaching patient problems. This system is a sophisticated and elegant approach to gathering information, a powerful way to sort and categorize that information and most importantly, a method to transform that information into a detailed and accurate assessment of the problem that organically shows the way to a practical, actionable plan to solve it.

I began to use and refine this system with my private consulting and coaching clients, and my consulting reputation grew.

Question Two: What specific knowledge and skills do you bring to your business that will give you an advantage in your marketplace?

Lesson Three: Never give up.

The years immediately after I walked away from my final PA job were a little scary, to put it mildly, and I tried a lot of things to make money on the internet, with very few of them being successful at first.

But I didn't give up. I tried and tried and yes, I tried again. Finally, I stumbled upon something that worked, and I took that success and ran with it. Later, I read that perseverance is one of the traits of a successful entrepreneur, and I had that in spades!

Question Three: What can you do to increase your ability to bounce back after a setback?

Lesson Four: Don't lie to yourself.

I happen to be a very optimistic person, confident on most days that things will work out for the best. Sometimes though, I allow that optimism to get in the way of a realistic outlook about how things are at the moment.

As much as I resented working for someone else, having that accountability in place in the form of a boss was at times very helpful. As an entrepreneur, the proverbial buck stops with me, and I am accountable to no one but myself.

Learning to tell the unvarnished truth to myself about what is working and not working in my business has been invaluable. Only when I can see the truth of a situation am I in a position to do anything about it.

Question Four: What lies have you been telling yourself about your business situation?

Lesson Five: Money isn't everything.

This is an old lesson, but one I had to learn several times before I really got it.

Family connections are much more important than any amount of money. Those "golden handcuffs" in the form of a regular salary, vacation time, retirement plans and health insurance are not as durable as I thought. Even if the handcuffs felt solid to me, they were of my own making and as it turned out, I held the key all along.

And your golden handcuffs don't have to be the same as mine. Fear of letting people down, losing the approval of friends or family and the fear of failure are all strong handcuff material.

Although I certainly don't recommend walking away from one's job without a safety net, sometimes it takes an extreme wake-up call to reveal the location of the key to those handcuffs.

Question Five: What "golden handcuffs" are keeping you imprisoned?

Lesson Six: Get a mentor sooner, not later.

In retrospect, I should have gotten a business mentor much, much earlier than I did. This would have significantly shortened my learning curve and saved me a lot of pain and money.

I just didn't fully comprehend that investing in mentoring would have been so valuable. Instead, I plodded along, trying to learn everything on my own and wasting far more money on lost time and lost opportunities than if I had had the guidance of an experienced and knowledgeable mentor from the start.

Question Six: What are your reasons (or excuses) for not hiring a mentor?

Lesson Seven: Nothing can take the place of action.

Even though I was medically trained to take quick, decisive action on behalf of my patients, this was a harder habit to bring to my business. Even after I found strategies that would bring in cash, like many online entrepreneurs, I allowed myself to rest on my laurels until the next cash crunch made itself known, as it inevitably did.

Today, I'm proactive regarding my business cash flow, not reactive. As an entrepreneur, you must constantly be in action to grow your business.

Question Seven: What actions are you postponing that will start or grow your business?

Lesson Eight: Learn to look at problems as the challenges they are.

As much as we humans crave the comfort of certainty and security, in reality, there is no such thing. In today's economy, downsizing can suddenly come tumbling down on career professionals who thought their jobs were rock solid. With the crash of the stock market, people who thought they had bombproof retirement funds saw them go up in smoke as their money and sometimes their homes were lost literally overnight.

And, as I saw all too often from my vantage point in the Emergency Room, loved ones can be taken from us in the blink of an eye, and even our own lives are much more fragile than most of us know.

Things are no different in business. Many people go into business to escape a dead-end job, low pay or a bad boss, only to find they are faced with one problem after another in their businesses.

This is the nature of business. There are always daily problems to solve. This is both the challenge and the opportunity that comes with being in business for oneself.

When I was a PA, I learned to enjoy approaching my patient's problems in a systematic and orderly way. I've now learned to enjoy this approach to my business problems as well.

Question Eight: How do you approach problems, as worrisome emergencies, or as challenges to be solved as a natural part of life and business?

Lesson Nine: Listen to your heart and then take action.

One of the most important skills I used every day with my patients was listening, but when it came to listening and then acting on what my heart-voice was trying to tell me, I failed miserably.

And because I didn't listen, circumstances taught me the lesson anyway!

I noticed that my heart-voice spoke most clearly to me when I was relaxed and had my mind on something pleasant, such as when I was driving in the countryside, taking a hot shower or walking in the woods. These days, I set aside regular time for these kinds of activities, knowing that I'm giving my heart-voice a chance to be clearly heard.

Question Nine: What is your heart trying to tell you that you've been discounting or ignoring? What can you do so that your heart-voice has a chance to be heard?

I have great respect for the power of scientific knowledge to bring value to our lives. And I have also come to fully accept there are other ways of knowing, ways that are just as valuable as any method based on hard scientific research.

Listening to your heart is one of those ways. And while I may not ever fully understand how my heart-voice knows what I need to hear, I do know enough to pay close attention.

After all, it's the lessons I've learned from listening to my heart that have finally given me freedom and control over my own destiny.

I'll never stop listening.

About Ellen Britt
Award-winning Online Marketing Strategist Ellen Britt is the co-founder of Marketing Qi (www.MarketingQi.com), helping savvy women entrepreneurs develop the business strategies they need to get the success they want. Ellen specializes in mentoring her clients to envision their businesses strategically and then guides them to combine the results with a custom, highly leveraged business model designed to produce immediate cash flow and continued profits.

Drawing on her 22 years experience in emergency medicine, Ellen has honed her interviewing skills to a fine edge and has had the opportunity to interview many of the most well known names in internet marketing and self-development. Her training has also given her the gift of a precise, systematic way to analyze and solve business problems. She's facilitated over a thousand of hours of teleclasses and is an expert at selling her high-ticket programs via preview teleseminars and in one-on-one phone conversations.

In addition to her two decades of experience as a physician assistant, Ellen holds a master's in psychology and a doctorate in biology. She's professionally trained in hypnosis and guided imagery and uses these skills extensively with her high-end clients to help them achieve breakthrough business results. Ellen lives and works near Atlanta, Georgia.

Trusting Feminine Energy in Business

Laura West

A couple of years ago I had my second annual astrology reading. My first reading was amazingly accurate as far as the timing of events and flow of income, so I was excited about the next one. I was planning to launch a big workshop in the fall and wanted feedback to know if the energy was aligned for the success of this workshop.

Well, according to the astrologer, the "stars" were not aligned with enrolling lots of people with ease for a big event during this time period. I thought to myself, "What am I doing? Am I trusting my marketing plan to the movements of the planets? Am I crazy?"

It's easy to trust a reading when it's all about expansion and abundance.

I really sat with this decision. I knew it was more than just deciding about holding this workshop. I was answering a question for myself about being willing to trust the flow of energy, signs and synchronicities from the universe and guidance from higher wisdom.

I had attended college for business. They didn't teach me about this energy stuff! But here I was making a decision that would impact the way I chose to run my business... from a deeper spiritual place and a trusting of higher wisdom that goes beyond just practical marketing plans.

I chose to trust.

I decided to let go of the idea of a big workshop. I was going to trust in energy flow and wrap my business around not only practical strategies, but also guidance that comes from a higher source.

Since I wasn't going to host a large workshop, I thought I would just put out this idea that I had in the back of my mind for some time that was niggling at me. I decided I would trust and host a small intimate workshop for ... Business Goddesses. While I'd been toying with the idea of a Business Goddess, I was also resisting it. "Business Goddess" felt a bit soft and too fluffy. I was afraid that women wouldn't take it seriously. Honestly, I was afraid that others wouldn't take **me** seriously.

Since I was committing to "going with the energy," I decided to *play* with this creative idea and not get attached to what would happen. I totally let go. I worked with a different graphic designer. I let him create a new look, and I didn't overly stress about it. I just had fun with the process. When I wrote the sales page, I let out my passion for women embracing their whole selves - their feminine energies of collaboration, love, creativity, freedom and their masculine energies of action, commitment, focus and risk – without worrying if I was doing a sales page "right."

The key to pay attention to here is "the idea that just wouldn't go away." I was resisting simply because of fear of what others would think. I chose not to worry about filling a big event and let it be what it was going to be. I had fun. I let go of over-thinking and let out my passion fully.

In the process, I easily attracted fifteen of the most amazing women to my three-day workshop.

Not only did I attract creative spiritual women to the event, five of them enrolled into a bigger seven-month group program with me.

Even bigger than all that…. I launched a whole new line of coaching programs and products for women entrepreneurs as Business Goddesses as a result of this small workshop.

Filling my coaching program and expanding my product funnel was just part of the success. During the workshop, these women had personal transformations that went beyond creating marketing plans. They tapped into a deep, knowing place about their inner creative powers, the gifts they were meant to bring to the world and absolute certainty that they were meant to do this work.

These women left the workshop with big shifts that seemed to move deeply into their very cells. I don't want to say that they weren't the same women who arrived at the hotel, but each definitely left a deeper, richer woman than when she came.

What I haven't shared with a lot of people about that workshop and about putting this "playful" idea out into the world is what happened for me.

To be blunt, I was flattened.

I literally couldn't work for several days. I couldn't focus for weeks. I found myself resisting marketing even though we had a campaign on the calendar. I felt physically ill at an event where they were selling tons from the stage. All of this resistance was not because of the effort it took in the workshop. The deep work we did was actually effortless for me.

What I know now was that the process was so transformational for these women that it was hard for me to take in. It was work that wasn't just about creating marketing strategies and plans. These women were profoundly changed and believed in themselves in a way that ran deeper than words can speak. They tapped into a belief about what was possible for them in their business success and that they really could run their businesses in a way that was absolutely in integrity. In fact, they received permission to run their businesses in a way that no one had ever acknowledged for them before. And they knew without a doubt that this was their right path.

It was so obvious I was on the right path, too, and yet it was hard to accept my own brilliance at work. I was amazed at how I was affected physically and emotionally. I was tired. My back went out for a month. I cried a lot. I was both scared of my innate power and excited about the possibilities. It took me a good six months to put anything out with Business Goddess on it.

I know we often get anxious over our plans and wonder, "When will success happen for me?" I received such a reminder that sometimes we have to grow into ourselves—and then it happens.

This was the year that I hit multi-six figures in my business revenue. I know part of that success was me being willing to grow personally so that my business could also expand and grow bigger, richer, and deeper.

What else did I learn? When you let go and play.... when you commit and yet let your passion and deep beliefs out and not be attached to the results... that's where the real juice is. This is where your soul gets to speak through you and through your business.

Sometimes we try so hard to get our ducks in a row that we miss what really makes our marketing powerful and magnetizing - letting our creative spirits speak through us.

You don't have to have the perfect words, the "right" sales page or elevator speech. Sometimes you can be packaged too perfectly, and there's no way for people to really get in. They need the realness of you.

At this time, I had been in business for about eight years, so I knew I was working my way toward a very big shift. I had put out a lot of joyful marketing, but still hadn't really let my soul speak. And that was what Business Goddess was and still is all about.

Even though the concept of Business Goddess was fun and light, I really had a huge resistance to it. It was very personal. I knew in many ways that I had been on this path my whole life - owning my power, daring to let my creative spirit shine through in my life and business and eventually, daring to claim that business could be different than when I worked in corporate. There IS another way of being in business that honors the feminine spirit along with much needed masculine qualities.

The big leap for me was to take my own idea seriously enough to play with it and put that idea out into the world. At first, the idea of Business Goddess was so scary because I was afraid of what others would think. What if they considered it too feminine?

I knew that two things had to happen. First, *I* had to take the idea of honoring the feminine seriously, and second, I had to be willing to put it out there for the world to see. For me, the only way I could release the idea was to let myself play and not get overly attached.

A very sneaky catch-22!

I know this has been part of my lifelong path of honoring the feminine inside of myself, while also honoring those masculine qualities. The masculine is revered everywhere around us, so it seemed easier to shore up my power by taking risks, making quick decisions, being persistent, and being focused. I tried my whole career to be like that.

It wasn't until I let out the idea that I resisted — giving it air, sunshine, and a place to be nurtured — that I started to see big leaps in my business growth!

My favorite lessons for accessing your courage, creativity and confidence to turn your ideas into income along this entrepreneurial path include…

1. Cultivate Your Creativity

In your business you are constantly being called on to use your creativity. You write articles and blog posts, create content for programs, write sales pages and marketing materials, design workshop experiences and tele-classes, create products, enroll clients, and constantly answer questions and make decisions.

You rely on your creativity every moment of every day.

With all this constant "delivering" of creativity, you need the space, time and a place to nurture and cultivate your new ideas. You may plan daily time away from the computer and your home office so you can hear those ideas that are waiting to be born. Plan retreats for a day, weekend or even a full week to create the next year of your business or work on your new big project. This creative expansion is not work to be done in between calls. It needs nurturing. It needs space to breathe and new perspectives to inform you of what wants to evolve through you in your business.

I know you may feel like you should be in your office ticking items off your to-do list. There's a time for that, too, but if you don't provide space to cultivate your ideas, then you'll never really put out work that speaks from your soul. It takes practice to create from your soul and to let your soul speak through your business.

2. Be Kind To Your Ideas

Think of your ideas as little sprouts from seeds you have planted. You wouldn't yell at them to "Grow now! Grow now!" You wouldn't say terrible things like, "What's wrong with you? You haven't sprouted a blossom yet! I thought we'd have yellow blooms by Friday at noon!" or "You're so demanding! What? You want more sunshine? Again?"

And, yet, we say these types of things to ourselves all the time. Ideas need time to incubate and marinate. It's ok to write down an idea and let it sit. Maybe the next week you mindmap the concept further; then you might start talking about it. Let the idea grow and evolve. You want to be committed and also patient and compassionate. You'll be rewarded with ideas that take shape into sturdy beautiful blooms.

3. **Not All Ideas Are Meant To Be Birthed**

When one of my clients heard this concept, she sent me an email and said that she felt so relieved! Just because you think you've discovered a good idea doesn't mean you have to implement it now or even at all. Sometimes ideas are just stepping stones to the next idea. Sometimes they aren't ripe yet and need time to marinate. You'll know when an idea is meant to be put into action... you won't be able to stop it or yourself!

You'll have so much natural energy to infuse in the idea that the action-taking will be easy!

4. **Make It Part of Your Process to Pilot**

Stop second guessing your idea. Be willing to share your thoughts and get feedback. Write about your idea and see what your community thinks about it. Send it to a few clients and get their reactions. Run a pilot workshop.

My favorite strategy is to put my new idea into a tele-class and see how my community responds. I'll know right away if there's energy and excitement around it. You can also offer your new program or product at a lower price so you can lead it one time. Then once you've gone through it, you can change anything that needs tightening up or add whatever is missing. Then you can raise the price and launch with great testimonials.

Your idea doesn't have to launch ready-made and perfect! You'll actually create a better product, run a more successful workshop if you share, test or pilot the concept first.

5. Resistance, Doubt and Confusion Are Signs of Growth

If you are experiencing resistance, doubt or confusion, then it's a great sign that growth is right around the corner. It means that something needs to shift for your business to evolve to the next place. Trust this, acknowledge where you are, feel your way through it, and be willing to take a baby step so you can move into the next phase.

6. As You Grow, Your Business Grows

If you are feeling frustrated with your business growth, then it's a sign that it's time for YOU to grow. You need to let something go, and step into the next bigger, bolder version of you. Your business will expand at the rate you grow.

This might look like putting out an idea that scares you a little (or a lot), like I did with the Business Goddess concept. It takes courage to put new ideas out into the world and let people look at them and "judge" with their pocketbooks.

7. Practice Deep Listening

Your ideas aren't born from your brilliant mind alone. We are all connected, and as you practice the idea of deep listening, you will hear or even see what idea wants to be born next.

Ideas come as answers to problems you are seeing with your clients, common frustrations you hear them repeating over and over, or maybe the trend that *you* are feeling. You have to spend time listening to what is really going on.

I encourage my clients to keep a running journal of what they are hearing, seeing and experiencing with their clients, potential clients and community.

There is a wealth of wisdom you can tap into, but you have to be willing to stop thinking you already have the answer and pay attention to what others are saying.

Notice what your clients seem to want and what they're already buying. What are your beginner clients saying, and how is that different from the issues your seasoned clients experience?

By practicing Deep Listening, you'll hear phrases, real language and situations that concern your clients, and these insights will be magic when you incorporate them into your products, your classes, and even in your marketing copy.

8. Trust Your Higher Wisdom

One of the challenges with trusting your higher wisdom is that it's easy to trust when times are abundant, expanding and prosperous. The real challenge is to trust when it feels risky, unknown, or it's not what you are expecting.

As you practice trusting your intuition, higher wisdom or divine guidance, you will feel more confident in your decision-making. You'll realize that you can actually rely on this wisdom throughout your day and as you plan your business.

9. Examining Your Money Beliefs

To complete the cycle of getting an idea and turning it into income, you'll need to examine your beliefs around money. If you do all the right things and make your idea tangible but don't think you deserve money or feel bad charging people for your services, then you'll block the flow of prosperity. I guarantee you'll find a way (consciously or not) to sabotage your success. It's like being in a hotel and calling room service to order dinner and then putting the "Do Not Disturb" sign out.

Business owners usually have the most limiting beliefs around marketing and money. To truly take your idea and build a successful business upon it, you'll need to take a look at these beliefs and shift them to empowering beliefs, ones that support your success.

10. Stop Trying To Do It Alone

Launching and growing a business is really a spiritual journey. It will call upon your deepest resources of time, money, effort and a sense of spiritual strength. It's too hard and confusing of a path to attempt to build your business alone. You want to assemble your Success Support Team as you go.

Your Success Support Team involves everyone from a business coach who believes in growing a successful business in a way that resonates with your creative spirit to virtual assistants, web masters, and business managers. Your biggest job is to keep a clear path for yourself so that you can put your work into the world. If you're bogged down doing behind-the-scenes maintenance, organizing or routine systems, then you aren't putting your genius work out there, and there are people in the world who won't get to work with you.

Your ideas start as precious little seeds. It takes daily courage to nurture your ideas and put them into action. It's only through putting your ideas into action that you will create a business that changes lives and achieves financial success. Finally, it takes trust. Trusting what your soul has to say – and letting it have a voice in your business.

About Laura West
Laura is the Founder of the Center for Joyful Business, JoyfulBusiness.com. and IAmABusinessGoddess.com. As a certified business coach, author and speaker, she is passionate about helping women create success lifestyle businesses filled with creative spirit, authenticity and prosperity.

Ms. West is the author of several information products including: *Business Goddess's Guide to Creating Powerful Sales Pages* and the popular *Joyful Business Guide*™, a creative business plan for your business using law of attraction principles.

She is a contributing author to four books for women entrepreneurs and is also the author of the upcoming book, *Awaken Your Inner Business Goddess.*

Find out more about her business resources, teleclasses, retreats and coaching programs at www.JoyfulBusiness.com.

Broadway, Broadcasting And Business

Shannon Cherry

"Without leaps of imagination, or dreaming, we lose the excitement of possibilities. Dreaming, after all, is a form of planning."
— *Gloria Steinem*

Ever since I was a kid, I've known what I wanted to do with my life. I knew my dreams and felt confident that I had the talent and tenacity to make them come true.

Along the way, I learned that you also need plans, strategies and back-up plans to make those dreams a reality. As I pursued my own plans, I discovered that the best way to use my talents didn't lie in my original dream. My dreams have evolved as my life has changed. My mission, however, has always stayed the same. In fact, my calling has only grown stronger through all the changes in my life.

I was going to be a Broadway actress. Ask anyone who knew me as a child. Acting had been my mission since the age of six. (Before that I wanted to be the first female astronaut in space, but someone told me that Russian cosmonaut Valentina Tereshkova had beaten me to it five years before I was born.)

Although my parents supported and applauded my efforts, they were a bit more worried about me being a 'starving actor' while I waited for my big break. So, as a senior in high school they asked me to put my dream 'on hold' while I created a backup plan – aka college. And there was one caveat: although I could participate in any music or theatre program, I had to choose a course of study that would pay my bills while I cut my teeth on the audition circuit.

And they were right. I wasn't a dummy by any means, and it would be nice to have a place of my own in New York City, instead of sharing 500 square feet with 3 other people!

It was one of my first lessons about dreams: they need to be realistic. And I've carried this lesson with me throughout my life. Dreams are wonderful! But they're more likely to become reality when backed up with a plan.

My parents helped me get real about my desire to be an actress by asking me some tough questions. What would happen when I had to choose between food and heat while waiting for an acting gig to come through? That's when I got innovative with my dream and started creating different techniques to plan for different situations.

How can you make sure a dream is viable? First, look at the concept from all aspects. Make a list of advantages and disadvantages. Mindmap. Journal. Use whatever tools you can find to unearth your ideas. Even ask others for their opinions. Sure, some will think you're crazy, and that's good to hear.

Of course, my parents were right. Broadway would still be waiting for me in four years.

So, after I received a full voice scholarship, I reluctantly agreed to go to one of the best state colleges in NY. I still had no clue what I would study, though (and frankly I didn't care).

The Evolution of The Big Idea

Once college was decided upon, all I had to do was sit back and coast through the rest of my senior year in high school. But because I was on auto-pilot, I almost missed out on one of the best ideas of my life.

I was sitting in my advanced English class as our guest lecturer, the local TV anchor and news director (the first woman TV news director in the US), talked on and on about journalism.

Yawn! I opened my notebook to give the appearance I was taking notes, but I was really looking at some new sheet music I was learning for a national voice competition (which I won, by the way).

Every so often, I would look up at the speaker, smile and nod, just to add to the impression I was interested. (See? I told you I was an actress!) At one of those moments, I caught a snippet of what she was saying. She had promised her dad to study something more than technical theatre in college and decided to learn TV news and production. The choice would relieve her dad who was worried of supporting an out-of-work theatre techie and satisfy her need to work in a sort of theatrical way.

The idea was practically handed to me on a plate. I could study my craft by acting as a TV reporter. Plus, all that on camera time surely wouldn't hurt.

Can you imagine what would have happened if I had focused on the sheet music and looked up five seconds later?

Lesson learned: **Ideas are all around us, but they can be elusive creatures. We need to be on the lookout so that we can grab the right ideas before they pass us by!**

Today, I'm known for generating lightening fast creative ideas. But that's because I slowed down the process and listened to what was going on in my head. And you can learn how to do it, too.

1. To begin learning how you come up with ideas, you need to be in a peaceful state. For me, I found it in the shower. (I still get most of my ideas in the shower.) Others may find the light bulb going off just before they fall asleep or just after waking up. Still others prefer meditation.
2. Whatever the activity, be sure to have a pen and notebook handy. (OK, I realize a notebook in the shower is a bit silly, so just keep it close by for AFTER you dry off.)
3. Write down the ideas as they come to you.
4. Once you are done, look back at the ideas and decide what triggered each one. For me, it's listening - hearing words from other people (or in my head). You may find ideas triggered from a visual, or a smell or a taste.
5. Once you have determined how you brainstorm best, start focusing on that technique more when you need ideas. For example, I often talk through a problem to solve (by myself or with a trusted friend) and usually half-way through the conversation, I have several ideas to use.

Now thanks to my listening skills (and some great timing), I finally had a college major, which I declared within my first week on campus.

I still wanted to get to The Big Apple as soon as possible, and I heard that having an internship could lop off several required college credits at once. With that, combined with my previous credits earned in high school, I could have me graduate a year early.

During my first summer back home from college, I landed a broadcasting internship with the same woman who had inspired me to choose the major in the first place.

I enjoyed everything I was learning, and to my surprise, I was good at it – not just good at acting the part of a TV reporter – but really, really good at broadcasting. So much so that my news director said I had one of the best BS detectors in the business and could convince a magician to reveal his secrets. (As a matter of fact, I've gotten two magicians to share how they do their tricks!)

That's why within two months of my 4 month internship, she hired me. By the time I turned 20 years old, I was one of the lead TV anchors.

My original dream had morphed into something I felt was much more than entertaining. I was shaping people's thoughts and ideas. I was righting wrongs. I was revealing truths. No longer was I giving characters a voice, I was giving real people a voice and letting them be heard.

Lesson learned: Ideas can – and should - change as you change and grow as a human being.

Although some may disagree, holding on too tightly to an idea can actually inhibit you from other opportunities (or even better ideas).

Remember when having a flash website was a good idea? What happens now when you come across one? You're either annoyed with the loud music or bored with the time it takes for the site to load.

I'm not saying here to give up on your ideas (although if you DO have a flash website still, I do suggest ditching that!). Just make sure the idea still can work in the environment you create for yourself.

For example, as a TV anchor I had unusual hours; I was either working before dawn or until midnight. Such hours weren't very conducive to a 22 year old's social life. I wanted to travel more, but it seemed the more successful I was, the more I was stuck behind the anchor's desk.

So it was time for another change.

A Good Kick in the Pants

Fast forward a few years and I found my social life improved so much I got married. And to add more to my plate, I was starting an exciting new job at a new PR firm in the area in which we lived.

Maybe still blissed out from my wedding and honeymoon, at first I didn't notice just how miserable the staff at this firm really was. But within days, I found out why - the boss was a tyrant.

He believed in threatening, belittling, and verbally abusing his staff in order to get them to 'produce.'

Yet, he seemed to actually like me. I didn't get his tirades and name calling. I got cash bonuses for getting consistent media coverage across the country for a client.

One day, I was called into my boss's office to be on a conference call with a client. I was expecting another bonus, as the client had just appeared on Good Morning America for a successful program they were doing. Instead, my boss said, "Who the %&*#@ do you think you are?"

Usually I have a snappy comeback for such comments, but I was so stunned. I remained silent while my boss, in front of the client, began reaming me out for getting the client on ONLY one major news program. And then, he began to use every word (and then some) to describe me and my 'inadequacies.'

Now, after working in TV for so long, I thought I had heard every swear word combination in the book, but I found out I was wrong. This (in my opinion) very evil man was trying to embarrass, harass and intimidate me. I had a choice.

I left.

I walked back to my office in the middle of his tirade, while he followed screaming at me. I grabbed my purse and my plant from my office and kept walking.

I got in my car and drove away. When I felt safe, I called my husband, in tears. He tried to calm me down, but I was inconsolable.

We had been looking at houses and wanted a family. I felt a failure. And new jobs were few and far between in that economy. I had no idea what I was going to do. I was inconsolable.

My husband asked me to meet him for lunch. I certainly wasn't hungry, but I reluctantly agreed.

When I arrived at our favorite diner, he was sitting and smiling. He handed me a piece of paper on which he'd written a domain name.

He said that I could not only do what my stupid ex-boss did, but I had more talent and could do the job better. And more importantly, I could do it on MY terms. I could be the boss I deserved.

Lesson learned: Sometimes you can't see the best idea. You need a good ally to be your guide.

Having a partner to rely on is essential to your business success. I was lucky, as I had a very smart, very supportive husband. But your partner doesn't need to be a family member.

Throughout my years in business, I've consistently reached out to others. I've hired coaches. I have mastermind and accountability partners. All of them have helped open my eyes to opportunities I was not seeing or taking advantage of.

What I love about accountability partners is that they cost nothing but your time – and can be one of your best business assets.

This person is more than a sounding board or a "yes man" there only to agree with everything you say or do. Your partner needs to understand and evaluate you, your motivation behind your ideas, and how to get more from you.

So when looking for your own accountability partner, here's what I suggest:

1. Find a person who is at your same level or slightly above. If there is too big a difference between the two of you, the partnership ends up being unequal and fails.

2. Look for a partner whom you can trust and whom you admire as a business owner.
3. Set up a time to talk every week and stick with that schedule.

Back to Basics

Getting a domain was the easy part; the hard part was getting clients.

After struggling for more than a year in my business, I had had enough. My savings were tapped out, and I was determined not to use a credit card or a loan to fund my business. (And I still haven't to this day! Everything is paid for by cash.)

I was about to give up on my idea and go back with my tail between my legs to the job market when something amazing happened.

I became pregnant… with twins. Instead of completely panicking, I saw succeeding in business as my mission. There was no way I could fail if I wanted to be home for my kids. I needed this business to be a success – and quickly.

Call it getting the nest ready, or just plain craziness, but I began rereading and going over all the thousands of dollars of 'stuff' I bought over the past few years, looking for the answer to home business success.

I couldn't find the insights anywhere. So I began throwing out all the material I had purchased. When I was done, 6 garbage bags had been filled.

I looked at my accumulated bags of knowledge and asked why would I waste money like this? It hit me. The answer was the why!

You see, it's the WHY I decided to invest in these how-tos, blueprints and programs in the first place. It was the same reason I wanted to be a Broadway star so many years ago.

The WHY was that these people had built a powerful presence – one that made me want to get to know them, like them and trust them. *A presence so powerful that it made me feel like buying from them was the right thing to do.* Then I realized, by using the skills I already had – and testing what worked for my target market – **I could build a presence** like those from whom I had purchased.

Lesson learned: **You can have great ideas, but no one will know about them if you don't tell them.**

You need to face facts: no matter what you do as an entrepreneur, you are a marketer first and foremost. This tidbit was tough even for me to swallow at first. The sooner you realize that no matter what business you're in, you're also in the business of marketing yourself, the better.

Because if you don't prioritize marketing, you will have no business.

Marketing is not just advertising nor does it involve implementing used-car sales techniques. It is the study of:

- why your clients buy your services
- what services they buy, when and how they make buying decisions
- what they are willing to pay for those services
- what would make them buy more
- what other products or services they want from you
- what causes them to defect and what causes them to stay with you.

In short, it is the essential understanding of how your cash register rings.

Once I realized this truth about marketing, everything got easier. I created the plans and the systems to market myself. And guess what? I got more customers and made more money. And now, I work less than I ever had to working for others, so that I can spend time with my wonderful twin daughters.

It All Comes 'Round Again

One lesson I learned early when I wanted to be an actress was that even though talent was important, connections make your career. The same concept was essential to my job as a TV anchor/reporter, as well as a PR professional.

And the same holds true for my business.

I created Be Heard Solutions to teach people how to build real relationships with their audience online and offline. I help coaches, consultants and entrepreneurs get their messages out to their targeted market.

It's another lesson I learned along the way. And it all boils down to three simple, yet powerful steps:

- **Find your voice.** Identify your ideal clients and know how to speak with them in the way that makes you an expert. This task involves more than just naming a target market, it's learning how to speak their language!

- **Tell your story.** Create content that establishes you as the go-to person for what you do. The key is to be true to your own principles and skills while making them relevant to your audience.
- **Be heard.** Send out your content via paths in which your ideal client will best see and hear your message. Knowing exactly what to do here will increase your traffic and visibility, attract more clients, and multiply your profits!

Little did I know those three steps would be the keys to the next stage in my life.

You see, my twin girls are diagnosed with autism. Although we're lucky to live in a state that offers a ton of support and services, it's still a struggle to get what they need to succeed in life.

Like many on the autism spectrum, they have language and communication barriers. Or to put it another way: they have a hard time finding their voice, telling their story and being heard. Although that had been my business motto long before the girls were born, it was quite some time after they were diagnosed that I realized my business motto was also my life mission. The same principles and skills I use for my clients and customers I now use for my girls. My role is to be the best possible advocate for them so that they can get what they need to succeed.

Lessoned learned: **You need to know the reason WHY you are in business if you want to reach your goals.**

The reason you are in business is never about money. Money may be the means to the real why, but it is never the why.

So take some time and think... really think about why you are in business for yourself. The reason is more than "money", and it's more than "helping people."

My why is for my girls. My business name is BE HEARD Solutions. My daughters, who arrived two years AFTER the business, have autism. I pursue this business with a passion to show them there are many different ways to be heard. And that's what I help my clients and customers accomplish as well... I use my talents and tenacity to help other people get their messages out.

Find your voice, tell your story and be heard. It's why I moved from dreams of the stage to a career as TV journalist and why I switched from TV to public relations. But now it's not just a business anymore... it's my life's work. And in some ways, it ALWAYS has been.

About Shannon Cherry, APR, MA

Imagine being the go-to person in your field... the expert your prospects want to do business with... the one everyone is talking about... the one getting more money consistently. Now imagine being that successful with authenticity and integrity... in a way that you build lasting relationships with those you serve.

Shannon Cherry, Your Creative Relationship Marketing Expert, helps you do just that by creating a powerful presence to make more money. Her background as a PR and marketing pro, as well as a TV reporter and anchor, combined with a unique ability to see through the clutter, gives her the expertise to build your exposure, increasing your credibility and visibility.

For more than 18 years, she has helped businesses increase their traffic, fill seats in programs and get more profits. Shannon has helped her clients appear in Parents, NewsWeek, Entrepreneur, USA Today and the New York Times, as well as on The Today Show, Fox News, The History Channel, CNN and The Oprah Winfrey Show.

She founded Be Heard Solutions in 2002 to help helped experienced and ambitious, entrepreneurs, coaches and consultants to create and grow the business they desire– without compromising on their sincerity and principles.

She proudly walks her talk: Shannon's business has been debt-free since its inception and she consistently works only 25-27 hours per week to spend more time with her family in the capital of New York.

Learn more about how to find your voice, tell your story and be heard with Shannon's free Be Heard! marketing pack at www.beheardsolutions.com

THE LIFE JOURNEY OF A SERIAL ENTREPRENEUR

Janis Pettit

I've always been a creative idea person. That's a right-brained thing. I've also been good at math and organization. Those are left-brained things. I guess I'm lucky to have that balance, because it takes both to turn ideas into income. I didn't always have that balance, though; I had to learn it. However, following my heart was not a choice but a must. I just knew all those years ago that I had to "do my own thing" and choose work that gave me satisfaction and joy. Coming from an entrepreneurial family, I had it in my blood.

Right out of grad school I followed my years of training as a singer and plunged headlong into a career as a New York actress. Just like any young "wanna be," I had stars in my eyes and no idea of what it would take to succeed and turn my dream into reality. My dream was just to perform and get paid for it. I wasn't even interested in stardom. No budding Lady Gaga with a burning desire for fame, that's for sure!

I plodded along, going to audition after audition, struggling to get into the unions, Actors Equity, SAG and AFTRA *(American Federation of Television and Radio Artists)* so I could make decent money and get some benefits. You couldn't get in without a union job, and you couldn't get a union job unless you were in - a true "Catch 22." But after a few years, I got a break. Someone hired me for a commercial and gave me my AFTRA card, which meant I was then eligible to join the ranks of the chosen and pay my dues to become a member of the other two.

I ended up doing musicals in New York and on tour, cabaret, TV commercials, soap operas and even cruise ships, but it was like being on a treadmill going nowhere. Each time a job ended, I was back to square one. My dream became frustrating. One day my mentor, Maxine Marx, a formidable casting director and daughter of the comic legend Chico Marx (the Marx brothers), said something I'll never forget. She told our small group that we were each like "a bar of soap on a supermarket shelf full of hundreds of bars of soap." In other words, if we didn't stand out, we just wouldn't get work.

Although this definitely wasn't an ego booster, it dawned on me that this whole show biz thing might be about marketing. I didn't know much about marketing, but I figured I'd better learn.

Lesson #1: You've got to master marketing. You can have the best product in the world, but if no one knows about it, or if it's not presented in a way that grabs attention, you won't succeed.

At about the same time, my heart was telling me that I had many other talents that were never going to be used if I stayed on this path, and I knew I had little power to control my destiny in the world of show business. The odds were probably 1 in 1,000 that I would really create the life and income I wanted, so I made the difficult decision to move in a new direction.

Lesson #2: Know when it's time to cut your losses and move on. Let go of your emotional attachment to any part of your business that's not working, and try something new.

One day a friend of mine who was a lawyer with the New York District Attorney's office asked me if I was willing to coach him on presentation and acting skills so he could improve his courtroom performance. That sounded like fun, so I said yes. We had a blast, and he loved the results, so he referred a few friends. Before I knew it, I had a little business.

At this point I would say I was like a leaf blowing in the wind, going where I was led. I hadn't made a conscious decision to go in this direction, it just presented itself. Before too long, I became friends with a woman who had a corporate job in Human Resources and who regularly developed and delivered training programs. We decided to start our own corporate training business. She specialized in assertiveness and compliance training (her expertise), and I concentrated on presentation and speaking skills (my background). This was my first plunge into the world of the small business owner. And we were home-based when you never told anyone you worked from home.

Lesson #3: Be open to opportunities that present themselves unexpectedly, even if they're outside your comfort zone. They just might be leading you toward your purpose.

Since this was pre-Internet, the only ways to market were direct mail, cold calling, networking or referrals, so it wasn't easy, and it was costly. And in spite of the fact that I came from a family of entrepreneurs, I still knew little about real marketing strategy. In fact, I was where many of my clients are today when they come to me. I had the skills to deliver a great service, but I knew next to nothing about getting clients and running a business.

Lesson #4: To turn your ideas into significant income, you need to also learn how to run a business. This is a different skill set.

Thanks to my partner's corporate contacts, we got sales appointments and gained contracts with some Fortune 1000 companies. They were happy with our work, and we got repeat business. But the truth was that we really didn't know how to turn our little business into a sustainable one. Maybe we would have gotten there, but her fear about the insecurity of not having a regular paycheck and benefits made her decide to return to the corporate world. I continued on by myself for a year or so, but was yearning to move out of the city to a quieter, greener place.

Finally my husband, a chef from Italy, and I made a decision to pursue a dream we had—to move out of the city and open an upscale Northern Italian restaurant—not an easy thing to do. We made a killing selling our New York condo apartment and chose a great location about 30 miles away, right across the street from the world headquarters of IBM. I committed to working with my husband for a year to get the business off the ground, and then I intended to go back to corporate training and coaching, about which I had become passionate.

This is where my real learning curve began. This is when I started learning how to be a successful entrepreneur.

By this point I had studied marketing and learned a few things. My husband ran the kitchen and I ran the business, including managing our staff, the marketing, the finances and the front of the house. In the first year we learned so much. We made a lot of mistakes, but the tide really turned when I began listening to what my customers wanted, and I began to use my creative ideas in my marketing. I watched what successful competitors did but tweaked it to fit our brand. I spoke with friends who had really successful restaurants in Manhattan. If you can make it there, you can make it anywhere! Within a few years, our marketing approach took us from a low 6 figures in sales to 7 figures. I got written up in the New York Business Journal for my creative marketing approach. A few restaurants even hired me as a consultant, and we consistently got 3-stars in the New York Times. Our clients were household names; celebrities and high level CEO's. I abandoned my idea of leaving because I knew that the business wouldn't work if I wasn't there. We were having a blast!

Lesson #5: Learn from people who have achieved the success you want, but put your own unique spin on it so you stand out. Use your creativity in your marketing to do this.

Lessons are often learned the hard way, and ours presented itself in our seventh year when suddenly the competition became fierce. The group of loyal customers who had come two or three times a week slowed to a few times a month as they tried the newest restaurants. We had the seven-year itch, a problem many restaurants face in trendy locations. We agonized over what to do and it finally dawned on me—we didn't have a plan. We had absolutely no growth strategy, no strategy to keep our customers coming back, no strategy to stand out from the growing crowd. Our sales were really taking a hit and we faced a hard choice—expand and open a second place while updating our existing location, expand our catering business, or sell and move onto something else.

Lesson #6: Don't ever take success for granted. You need to have a well-thought out strategy to turn your ideas into multiple streams of income. (I help clients do this with my 6-Figure Business Design Model™.)

They say "strike while the iron is hot," so we decided to sell while we could still get a good price. In fact, we'd been talking for several years about the appeal of moving to a warmer climate where the cost of living was more reasonable. So we researched our options, sold our home and my husband, daughter and I moved to Raleigh, North Carolina. It was scary to move away from the New York area and all of our friends. It was a leap of faith.

At this point, to be quite honest, I was really yearning to return to coaching and training, but I was in a new city with no business network. So instead, I purchased an existing business, which turned out to be a big mistake. It was a small company that published and distributed a magazine for new homeowners. It was an irresistible deal, and I saw the money potential. But the mistake was that I wasn't the least bit passionate about what I was doing. I didn't look forward to work each day; in fact, sometimes I even dreaded it.

I added direct mail services, but the majority of the sales came from advertising revenues. And guess who the head sales person was — me! Over two years I tripled the sales and actually franchised the business for other markets. Finally, with the help of a business broker, I sold the whole thing a few years later.

Lesson #7: You can make money without being passionate about what you do, but it won't bring you joy. Passion is what keeps you going, even if the going gets rough, which it does at times. Plus, people who are passionate are usually giving back in a big way.

I was discouraged. I wanted to return to my dream of owning a coaching business, but I didn't have the confidence that I would succeed, because it was a different sort of business than I'd had before. I really wanted to take all I'd learned as a successful entrepreneur - knowledge that corporations used to pay me thousands of dollars to deliver in training programs - and make it available to people like me - passionate small business owners. I just wasn't sure how to pull it off.

I guess the Universe took over, because I attended a big luncheon for women in business where the guest speaker was acclaimed life coach Laura Berman Fortgang. Her background was eerily similar to mine, and she'd become a huge success, appearing on Oprah and CNN. Something shifted inside as I heard her speak. It was like a wave of yearning and clarity passed through me. Afterward I spoke privately with her and told her of my fears. Could I do this? How could I build a coaching and speaking business, which would involve some travel, and still be a great mom to my young daughter? I knew she had young children and wanted to understand how the heck she managed it all. She took my hand and looked in my eyes and asked if I knew this was the path I wanted. I answered yes. She told me I needed to go for it and that I could build my schedule and my business around my life.

That was a true "aha" moment. I could have a lifestyle business? Wow!

Lesson # 8: Turning your ideas into income means you can create a business that can be built around the lifestyle you want to live. TIP: When I plan out my yearly calendar of coaching programs and live events, the first thing I do is block off time for my vacations and family holidays!

I started my coaching business in 2002. I had the ideas in my head of how I could help small and solo business owners succeed, but it took a lot of struggle to turn it into income. First, I started speaking locally and getting clients that way. But the first year I made under $20,000. I didn't know what to do. At this point I started learning from some Internet marketers. This was a whole new marketing world, and I began to see that if I really learned how to reach people online, I could reach thousands. Over the next few year two major shifts happened for me.

Shift #1: I realized I needed a coach who could teach me how to use the Internet to grow my business.

Shift #2: I became aware that for some reason I had completely abandoned what I knew about the importance of having a solid business strategy and about creative marketing. I realized I had to go back to what I knew and use it in my new business.

Shift #3: After working with a mentor for a while and undergoing a huge learning curve, I realized I needed to get my knowledge out of my head and transform it into information products, templates, systems and processes that would increase my income and make learning easy for my clients, which leads me to…

Lesson #9: You must get your ideas out of your head and turn them into a logical sequence of information products, programs, systems, processes and deliverables that get results for your clients if you want to generate the passive and recurring income necessary to provide you with a solid 6-figure income.

For the sake of brevity, I won't go into all the details, but slowly my business grew. It wasn't overnight, and I give true credit for my big breakthroughs to the wonderful mentors I had over those years. But then life threw me a curve. In late 2005, my husband was suddenly diagnosed with Stage 4 kidney cancer. He had been a smoker and had not caught the early symptoms of the disease. My world was turned upside down as I put my business in a holding pattern and tried to hold down the fort, caring for a then-11-year-old daughter and a gravely ill husband. In just five short months, he was gone. We had been married for 25 years.

To be honest, I was overwhelmed and scared. How could I deal with the terrible grief my daughter was suffering, my own grief and the overwhelming task of being the sole provider? I started adding up the cost of braces, college, mortgage and all of the other living expenses we all have. Could my ideal business actually give me the income I needed for years to come?

After a lot of soul searching and with the support of my family and friends, I took a realistic look and realized that not only was my income already enough to support us, but also I had the skills to continue to grow and evolve my business. I started to gain a new level of confidence and sheer determination to do what I loved, to commit to helping others in a bigger way, and to create a generous income and comfortable lifestyle for myself and my child.

Lesson #10: Life will get in the way. You can count on it. But if you are called to do what you do, if you've been given big ideas for a reason, if you know in your heart that this is your path, then don't let life's setbacks stop you. Go get the help and support you need.

Since that difficult time in 2006, my business has exploded. I've created new and better programs, I've implemented new ideas, and I've been able to help hundreds of small and solo business owners to make more money doing what they love. I'm a lifelong learner. I'm always learning new technologies, marketing tactics, strategies and techniques I can use to help my clients.

Most importantly I'm living the life I want. We spend time each year in Italy, which I adore. I take my daughter to New York to the theater and museums. I have time to devote to helping others. I'm living my best life, not every day and not always in every way, but most of the time.

I'm blessed to be able to be who I was meant to be.

About Janis Pettit
Since 2002, Janis Pettit has helped hundreds of small and solo business owners worldwide achieve their entrepreneurial and lifestyle dreams. Her focus is on helping micro lifestyle business owners.

Janis currently lives in Raleigh, North Carolina with her adored teenage daughter Julia, who makes sure she doesn't become hopelessly "uncool." She speaks Italian fluently and loves traveling to Italy to visit friends and family. Her well kept secret is that she is an accomplished classical singer who sang professionally for a number of years and she continues to sing for pleasure. Visit her online at http://www.smallbusiness-bigresults.com

Sometimes Things Get Worse Before They Get Better

Michele Pariza-Wacek (PW)

There are some people who decide to follow their hearts and everything falls into place beautifully.

I am not one of those people.

I share this because in case you too are someone who decides to follow her heart and it takes a little while for things to click (and maybe even things get worse for awhile), it's okay. It doesn't mean you're not on the right path. It just means that the path is a bit bumpier than what you originally thought.

But I get ahead of myself. My story starts when I was 3 years old and taught myself to read because I wanted to write fiction so badly. I spent high school and college casting around trying to figure out how else I could make a living writing while I worked on my novels.

Everyone told me to become a journalist. That was the last thing I wanted to be, so I kept searching. And then, in college, I stumbled onto this entire world of copywriting.

So what is copywriting? Copywriting is writing promotional materials for businesses. It has nothing to do with protecting intellectual property or putting a copyright on something like a song or a piece of art (note the difference in spelling).

Now, before I go any further, let me explain this entire copywriting business. You see, there's a lot of writing that goes on in businesses. But most of it is not regular work, which is why a lot of writing is outsourced to freelancers rather than hiring lots of writers as employees. Hence there's this entire freelance copywriting industry out there.

I stumbled upon this industry pretty much by accident while still in college. Actually, it would be more appropriate to say freelance copywriting found me — jobs started flowing to me while I was still in college.

"This is great," I thought and immediately decided I needed to find a job freelancing.

The Universe, however, knew my path lay in another direction. So while finding freelance writing gigs was easy, finding an actual job was not.

But I was determined. I was sure I was supposed to be in a job. So I kept pushing it. And eventually I got my wish — I ended up landing a couple of agency jobs, a corporate job and a city government job.

But something didn't feel right. I was restless. It wasn't so bad for my first couple of jobs when I was still in Madison, Wisconsin, but I started getting VERY restless after I moved to Prescott, Arizona and got a job in the communications department of the City of Prescott.

This was 1998. I was pretty unhappy there but didn't feel like I could quit. My husband was in the middle of transitioning out of his first business, and I didn't think we could afford not having a steady paycheck. Worse, my relationship with my boss had been deteriorating over the past 6 months. Would I even be able to keep my job?

I took a couple weeks off to visit my family back in Wisconsin. My husband and I had decided I would quit when I returned, and I'd start freelancing again.

But then I got cold feet. My first day back I was all set to turn in my notice and then I thought to myself, "This isn't so bad. And isn't having a steady paycheck better than the uncertainty of freelance work?"

I called my husband to tell him I changed my mind and he actually got a little angry with me. He said, "I thought we decided you were going to quit. You're not happy, so quit."

I thought about it and realized he was right. So I went over to my boss's office and turned in my notice.

It was the best thing I could have done. I started my business in 1998, and fairly quickly I built up a pretty decent freelance copywriting business.

The biggest problem with it, though, was what I had built was a serious feast/famine business model.

What's a feast/famine business? Basically it means I would swing between having too many clients to too few — rarely did I ever have "just enough."

When I had too many, I was stressed because I was working all the time. And when I had too few, I was stressed because I wasn't sure how I was going to pay the bills.

How did I end up with this business? Because I would market like mad when I wasn't busy, and I would stop when I was. After all, there were only so many hours in a day. When I was busy, the first thing that would go was the marketing.

Between the stress of my feast/famine business and the fact the Universe wasn't through with me, in the fall of 2003 I realized something needed to shift. I started getting restless again. Something wasn't right.

At first I misdiagnosed what was going on. I thought my restlessness was because I wanted bigger jobs and to be making more money. I mistakenly thought if that happened, my feast/famine business model would go away. At the time I had mostly local clients. Perhaps I needed to go find bigger clients. And that led me to the Internet.

Now here's where it gets interesting. At the same time I started learning and educating myself on how to market myself on the Internet, my local clients started going away. And no new local clients came on to replace them.

At first I was happy. That MUST mean I was on the right path, right? And by having my local clients leave, that MUST mean I was about to get all these new bigger clients.

Right?

Well…

What followed was one of the worst periods in my business. For 6 months my business just died. I was barely making a thousand dollars a month. One client owed me about $300 and it took months to get paid. I was so stressed that I couldn't get that $300, it almost made me sick.

I became quite depressed. I had a lot trouble focusing or getting anything done. It would take me hours to complete simple tasks. I wasn't building any momentum. I was just sinking lower and lower.

It got so bad my husband finally looked at me one day and said "This doesn't seem to be working anymore. Are you sure you want to be doing this? Or do you think you should get a job?"

That stopped me. Quit? It never occurred to me to quit. Even though I was seriously depressed and stressed about how nothing seemed to be working, quitting had never been a part of the equation. I thought about that all night. What did I want to do?

And that's when I realized I wanted my own business. But somehow in this switch from local clients to marketing online I had lost my way. I wasn't doing everything I knew I should be doing. I had allowed my depression over the lack of work to color my entire life.

So I recommitted myself to my business. And less than a month later everything turned around. I landed a few big clients and ended up making up all my lost income in the second half of 2004.

However, the restless still didn't go away. What on earth was the problem? I was a freelance copywriter. I had the exact same business as other freelance copywriters. What was the problem? Why should I be restless?

It took another year for the answer to finally hit me. I was an entrepreneur, not just a freelance writer. Yes I am a writer. I need to be writing to be happy (I've written 2 novels) but my path is much bigger than what I can accomplish as a writer. I needed to transform myself into an entrepreneur and build a direct response copywriting and marketing business. Only by doing that could I begin to reach the number of people and help the number of business owners and entrepreneurs I was meant to help.

So how did I do it? Below are the 8 key steps.

1. I took Einstein's quote to heart. "The definition of insanity is doing the same thing over and over and expecting different results."

In December 2004, I made a horrible discovery. For some reason, I'm not sure why, I went through my QuickBook™ statements and started comparing how much I made each year. To my disgust, I discovered that I basically made the same amount of money each year ($40,000 to $50,000).

You see, over the years when I was in the "feast" cycle of my business, I would proudly tell people I was "growing" my business. Never mind the "famine" cycles were completely wiping out any gains from the "feast" cycle. I had also raised my rates over the years. And yet, nothing had changed. In fact, my best year was one of the years when my hourly rate was the lowest.

All of a sudden the realization hit me. I wasn't growing a business. I had reached a plateau and I was stuck there.

At about the same time I saw the "Seinfeld" episode where George decides he doesn't like his life right now (broke, jobless, living at home, no girlfriend), so he decides do things the opposite of what he always did. And it worked! By the end of the show he had a girlfriend and a job with the New York Yankees.

2005 became the year I did the opposite of what I always did. This leads me to the second tip.

2. I hired a coach or a mentor. Once I discovered that I was stuck, I realized that I probably needed some help getting unstuck.

You see, there are two issues going on. The first one is realizing you're the reason why you're in this situation in the first place. The second is actually doing something to change it.

And it's not as easy as it sounds to change things. Your perspective on yourself, your thoughts, your actions, etc. are cloudy at best. Now there's no question you can change things, but it's a lot more difficult without someone to point things out to you.

There are also some other benefits to hiring a coach or a mentor for yourself. When you do, you're telling yourself (and the Universe) that you're ready to take yourself seriously and do what it takes to be successful. You're also saying you're worth the investment. (Because that IS what you're doing — you're investing in yourself by getting coaching, mentoring and education from someone who has been there so you can get to where you want to go a lot faster and with fewer detours.)

Now you do need to make sure you hire the right coach or mentor — not all are created equal, so take a little time to make your choice. Don't just pick the first one. Do some research and ask around to make sure you pick the mentor who's right for you.

3. I made sure my business was the right entity for tax and legal purposes. I can tell you as soon as I incorporated, I felt like I actually had a business. There was something about going through that process that made me feel like I finally had a "grown up" business.

I'm not an expert on this, so what I would suggest is making an appointment with the experts (i.e. a CPA and an attorney) and discussing it with them.

4. I started attending events. Now, I'm not talking about becoming a seminar junkie. But I do believe going to events is key to taking your business to the next level.

There are so many benefits from attending conferences beyond what you're going to learn from the speakers — networking, connecting with your "tribe," getting out of your own little world so you can get some fresh ideas for your business, meeting the "movers and shakers" in your industry and more.

In addition to all of that, you also may discover your business starts to take off because you're finally taking yourself and your business seriously.

5. I started marketing regularly. This one is tough if you don't have a support system, but it's critical if you want to break the feast-famine cycle.

If you want to have a steady stream of clients and customers and a full pipeline of leads, the way to do that is by marketing consistently. It's that simple . . . and that difficult.

But there are two things you can do to make this MUCH easier. First, change your mindset so you put as much emphasis on marketing as you do everything else in your business. Then implement a system to make it easier for both you to follow through and your team to support you.

6. I got in alignment with what I taught. In my case, it meant making marketing my own business as important as marketing my clients' businesses. In your case it may look different. But the reality is, you personally need to be in alignment with what you teach, or how can you possibly stand tall and value your gifts and your brilliance?

The only way you're going to transform your business is if you do what you need to do to be in alignment and practice what you preach. If you're struggling, maybe you need to take a hard look at what you're providing. You might need to tweak your offering. This could be a message from the Universe you're not doing what you're truly meant to do.

7. I surrounded myself with the right people. You can't do it all yourself. If you want to grow your business, you need to get a team in place to support you. Now this is something else that can feel scary — after all, hiring people is a big commitment. So what I would suggest is start small. Hire a VA (virtual assistant) for a few hours a month or a bookkeeper. Then make sure you use that time for revenue-producing activities.

Eventually, you're going to reach a point where you have a big team working for you. The only problem with that is then you suddenly find yourself spending a bunch of time managing them. That's when you want to look into getting a COO or a business manager for your business. I was lucky. My husband has joined the business as the

COO and that has made a HUGE difference in being able to grow the business.

8. I did what I needed to do to work through my blocks. You may have heard the quote (and I'm paraphrasing) that the best self-development tool is having a business. ALL your obstacles and blocks will show up as you start and grow a business. And don't be surprised if some of the biggest blocks show up when everything looks good on the surface.

I have two suggestions. First, know this is normal and be prepared for it. Second, don't stop investing in yourself. Do whatever you need to do to keep moving forward and breaking through those blocks. Maybe you need a coach, a product, or something else. Or maybe you need to finally outsource something you've been reluctant to let go of (your copywriting for instance?)

Chances are you know what you need to do to keep moving forward, so what I want to encourage you to do is honor that feeling, start taking action.

9. I took action. Nothing happens if you don't take action. The best advice I can give you (other than marketing yourself regularly) is to get those to-do's crossed off your to-do list and watch your business grow!

Remember, the road CAN be bumpy. Just because you make a decision and start down a specific road DOESN'T mean all your problems float away. Remember, when my business died for 6 months, it was after I had made a decision to play a bigger game. There's no question looking back on this I WAS on the right path. But I needed to commit to it. I had still left myself an "out" — I could go back to my local clients and play my smaller game if the bigger game didn't work out. But playing a bigger game doesn't work out like that. I needed to be "all in" — and only when I did that did things finally turn around.

So just because things get bad after you decide to follow your heart doesn't mean you're not on the right path. You just might need to do something a little different or make a deeper commitment.

But there's one thing I can promise you. If you give up, you're never going to see your dream come true. So whatever you do, don't give up.

About Michele PW, Your $Ka-Ching$! Marketing Strategist
Imagine: Your potential customers transforming into actual customers…all without you lifting a finger. Sound too good to be true? It's not…when you hire Michele PW (Michele Pariza Wacek) Your $Ka-Ching!$ Marketing Strategist.

What Michele specializes in is writing copy and creating marketing campaigns that gets people to TAKE ACTION, whatever that action may be (signing up for your newsletter, buying a product, hiring you etc.). In fact, Michele has mastered psychological and hypnotic techniques designed to persuade your target market to become your customers.

She also specializes in warm Web 2.0 traffic strategies that will bring a flood of hungry visitors to your Web site who want to buy exactly what you sell!

Whether it's online or offline you need, Michele PW knows how to Rev Up Your Results!

Want to transform your web site into a cash machine? Michele PW is offering a free copywriting rescue kit at http://www.michelepw.com/freegift

WHAT IF THERE WAS NO BOX?

Brian Rooney

I've never been a traditional thinker. Bosses (back when I had bosses) and coworkers (back when I had a regular job) would often describe me as someone who "thinks outside the box."

The smartest bosses I had really valued my creative strengths. The other bosses were constantly frustrated with me and wondered why I couldn't think and act more within their parameters.

Those co-workers who valued my innovation would often come to me for creative problem solving or to look at an existing situation with a new perspective. That didn't mean my ideas were always implemented or even the best ideas available. Sometimes it just helped to have a different perspective on a given situation.

None of this is intended to imply that I live purely by instinct or by following only my heart. My own life experiences have taught me that both the head and the heart have their roles to play in making decisions in life and in business.

For example, our minds help us make decisions based on previous input and past experiences, both good and bad. When we were younger and touched a hot surface, a couple of things happened. First, we got burned! Secondly, we recorded a memory that reminded us not to touch a hot surface again.

Our minds can be tremendous assets. All those memories come in handy when we need to remember a phone number, someone's name, a process we've used successfully, a technique we've learned that has served us well, etc. But, if we're not careful, our memories can also become liabilities.

For example, when we face relationship issues, failed business ideas, or something that just didn't go the way we hoped it would, we not only feel the pain of that event but we also build an instant memory of what that felt like and how it happened. Our minds will often try to use those painful memories to protect us against future pain by constantly reminding us of the feelings of some past failure.

I believe this constant reminder is why so many of us fail to truly venture out and reach our full potential in every area of our lives. Others tell us, "You can't do it like that," or "That's not how it's done." Maybe a well-meaning friend or family member has told you, "Remember the last time you tried something like that."

No doubt, these friends and family members meant well. They didn't want you to experience failure or to get hurt. But there are times when I believe we have to move forward, because we just somehow KNOW that it is the right thing to do. I'll give you an example from my own business life.

It is important to understand that I have virtually zero college education. I say "virtually" because I actually did attend North Texas State for a number of weeks before dropping out to go on tour with a band. Everyone around me thought I was crazy and making a foolish decision. I just KNEW that this was the "right" move for me to make. I wanted to be on tour and spent the next two years traveling all over the country playing bass.

The other part of the story is that there was also a young lady who was following her heart and who had begun touring with a completely different music group. The assistant director on her tour was a very good friend of mine. When both our tours ended, he introduced me to this young lady. We've been married over twenty-three years, have five amazing kids and a beautiful grandson.

If I had followed traditional logic, it is entirely possible that I would have never met the woman who would become my wife. I can't imagine life today without her and our amazing family.

Of course, not completing college presented its own challenges. Those five kids liked to eat... several times a day! Life became very expensive, and I was holding down multiple jobs to survive.

My head, friends, family members, and even strangers were quick to pronounce my situation as hopeless. With no college education, there didn't seem to be a lot of options available to me. It would seem to others that my life was destined for many long hours at low paying jobs, just barely scraping by.

But there was something inside me that just KNEW there was a different path. I didn't have any idea what that solution was, but I completely believed that there WAS a way for me to rise above what looked like a desperate and hopeless situation.

While working one of my many jobs that I absolutely hated, I was surprised by a memory of a teacher from back in my high school days.

I was literally jolted in my chair by a sudden urge to look her up. A few phone calls later, I had found her number and placed a call.

I explained that I wasn't actually sure why I was calling other than I knew somehow that I was supposed to contact her. I asked if I could buy her lunch some day if she should happen to be in the area.

Here's the crazy part. She was actually on her way to the town where I lived at that moment. I had unknowingly called her on her cell. She wanted to meet me for lunch that same afternoon!

Logic or "traditional" thinking would say that it made no sense to even call her. I didn't really know WHY I was calling. I just knew I was supposed to look her up and make that call.

I asked the only question I knew how to ask at that time. "How does a guy like me get some sort of training to help increase my earning potential?"

We talked for a few hours and then said our good-byes. She had a few tips for me and said she would do some thinking and get back to me.

The next day, this former teacher called and offered me a job at her financial services company. She was also following her heart rather than her head with this call because logic and traditional thinking told her that she was hiring someone with no training, no experience, and no realistic expectation of success. But she also KNEW that this was the right call to make.

The short version of the story from this point forward was that I was able to exceed all the goals we set, and I learned how to make more money than I had ever made in my life up to that point.

The job was great, and she was an amazing boss. But, for me, there was something still missing. I was making great money, but I was almost never home. I was missing critical moments in the lives of my children. So I made the decision to begin working from home.

Again, my head was screaming, "What are you doing?!? You have a DREAM job!" Well-meaning friends and family members thought I was crazy. Many of them would have traded places with me at any moment. But I knew that I wanted to be home with my children. I didn't know how I could swing it, but felt something would work out, because my family had to come first.

There were a number of missteps along the way. I tried some business ideas that failed to produce the desired results. There were times when I felt like a failure. I had left a good job to be home and was now making less money. But still ... that "something" ... that "still small voice" ... that "intuition" was speaking to me to stay the course. There was a solution. I just had to keep moving forward.

Like many people, I had turned to the Internet to discover possibilities. I had started a little home-based business writing online business articles, doing some brokering for other financial service companies, playing a little music on the side and picking up various projects here and there.

Along the way, I was hit by another moment of inspiration for a service that I truly believed would help other home based business professionals like myself – an autoresponder service. I ran the idea by a small list of online subscribers to whom I had been sending my articles, and the response was literally overwhelming. I had people ready to order on the spot! But what I didn't have was the actual service to provide them.

I was great at sales but had no programming knowledge at all. And to make this idea work so that I could actually start charging customers, I needed to find someone who would create what I had envisioned. This was years ago when finding software developers was more of a challenge.

I had begun playing bass for a big band just twenty minutes from my house. I met the drummer at our first rehearsal, and we started getting to know one another. One day he invited me to lunch.

He knew that I worked from home and was somehow able to support five children doing so. He was looking at a possible career change and wanted to see if I had any ideas or input for him. We spent a little time talking about his particular areas of interest, what sort of income goals he had, etc. At some point in the conversation, I told him about this great idea I had.

I explained that I had people ready to start paying for the service, but I didn't actually have the autoresponder service yet. I told him, "What I really need now is somebody who can write the software to make this thing happen. I can sell it like crazy. I just need somebody to build it."

My new friend and fellow musician got a funny look on his face and said, "Didn't I tell you? That was my other major in college. I'll bet I could build that for you!"

My first thought was, "You have GOT to be kidding me!" Here was this drummer that I'd been playing music with for a while, and he actually had the skill set I needed to be able to start selling this service!

Not only did he build a prototype, but we were able to start selling the service within weeks. Eleven years later, we are the best of friends and business partners.

That little idea I had has become one of the most successful AutoResponder services online today. TrafficWave.net operates in over 140 countries. We provide autoresponder and ad tracking services to thousands of businesses in a broad range of industries. And it all started from a moment of inspiration when all I had going for me was "knowing" there was a solution. I just had to find it.

Over the years, I've launched other web sites and have created multiple streams of income. The Internet makes it possible for us to streamline, consolidate, outsource, and fine-tune our processes like never before.

The biggest piece of advice I share with people today is to simply trust your instincts and get started. That idea came to you for a reason. You don't have to know the full story. You really just have to get started.

I never knew the whole story when I started any particular project. Most of the time, all I had was an idea of what I wanted to do with no clue about how it was going to happen!

I make a point of bouncing my ideas off trusted friends, my wife, and advisors. I listen to what they have to say, and then I make my decision based on what I feel is right for me.

I can't tell you that every idea I've ever had was a wild success. Sometimes I learned more about what NOT to do when a particular idea didn't pan out the way I had hoped. But even those lessons were extremely valuable as I moved forward with other projects.

There are always adjustments to make along the way. Much of what we implemented eleven years ago with TrafficWave.net has changed considerably. My inspiration was simply the starting point to get things moving forward.

If you find yourself with an idea or an inspiration that sticks with you day after day, plays around in your mind while you try to sleep, keeps coming back even after you set it aside, consider giving the idea some room to breathe. See what steps you can take now just to get things started. Imagine what the completed project might look like and then begin filling in the spaces with action to make it happen.

You may be surprised at how some of the other pieces start to come together in completely unexpected ways to help you fulfill that vision.

Start by believing that there IS a solution. Then begin taking the steps to discover that solution. Don't be afraid to consider approaches that seem "outside the box." The reality is that there is no actual "box." We just have memories that are used to create the "borders" that we think define how life is supposed to be.

But remember … the best ideas, solutions, and opportunities are discovered when we're willing to ask, "What if there was no box?"

About Brian Rooney
Brian is the co-founder of TrafficWave.net LLC. TrafficWave.net provides AutoResponder and AdTracking services to thousands of clients from more than 60 countries. Request Brian's Free Report: "How To Boost Sales With AutoResponders online at www.trafficwave.net

CONFESSIONS OF A BEST-SELLING AUTHOR

Leslie Householder

In case you don't know me, let me introduce myself. I'm Leslie Householder, the award-winning, three time best-selling author with a successful and growing 6-figure business, helping families achieve prosperity. I am a mother of seven children, and while many people think I "have it all together," this peek behind the scenes will enlighten and inspire you as you're given a glimpse into the challenges I've faced even *after* my flagship story, *"The Jackrabbit Factor"* achieved international acclaim.

It was the major financial breakthrough for my family in the year 2000 where I'll begin. After seven excruciating years of hardship, and having lived in such desperation that I actually called the police on a kid who broke my broom, my husband and I learned some things that finally allowed our family's income to suddenly triple.

From that experience, my book, *The Jackrabbit Factor* was born - a story encapsulating our journey and revealing the secret behind our breakthrough. Within weeks it became a best seller, and has since been picked up by publishers around the world for translation into multiple languages.

I'm proud to say that this page-turner (which can usually be read in just one sitting) was a catalyst for facilitating similar breakthroughs in the lives of thousands of readers. Cited as a key factor in helping Ben Southall win the "World's Best Job" contest out of 34,000 applicants, the book was ultimately made available as a free download at www.jackrabbitfactor.com, which I'm grateful to say, has helped us build a worldwide following for *all* of my writings.

However...

Trust Your Heart - Even When the Short-Term Results Seem Disastrous

In spite of my tremendous success, it wasn't until the beginning of 2006 that the real life lessons began. With a list of ambitious goals, dreams, and the passion and intention to see them through, and with too many good opportunities showing up to do proper due diligence on *any* of them, my husband and I felt it was time to take the leap of faith to have him leave his job and become a full-time investor *and* help me with my seminar business.

Our plan? Take *The Jackrabbit Factor* to New York Times bestseller status - the holy grail of all best-seller lists - that summer. We knew it would require rigorous campaigning, and with six kids at home (at the time), I knew I wouldn't be able to accomplish it without my husband's help and computer expertise.

However, in February of that year, I discovered I was expecting baby number seven. We always knew that we wanted one more, but *this* baby's timing was much sooner than expected.

Now, one thing I will tell you is that when I'm pregnant, I am NO fun to be around. We've joked many times that on the day that the kid broke my broom, *I lost my mode of transportation.*

Besides being no fun to be around, I also lose all interest in doing anything business-related. As far as I'm concerned, I'm DONE, and I don't care if it all falls apart.

(Remember, my husband just quit his job to help me take the book to NY Times. And suddenly, I've gone to bed, hating the world, hating my business, and mad at my husband for not having an income.)

With this new development in our lives, we both wondered WHY we had felt so RIGHT about taking the leap at that time.

In hindsight, I understand. But in the middle of it, we both felt like our whole world was crashing down.

To hold things together, we lived on savings and my husband started earning commissions finding people to rescue who were in pre-foreclosure. He went door-to-door and showed people how to stay in their homes and earned pretty good commissions doing something completely out of his comfort zone. This lasted nearly a year.

At the end of 2006, we bought spec homes for a quick profit. Within a couple months it became clear we had made a big mistake. We carried those homes for nearly a year while we waited for them to sell. It was during that year that I began to blog again, for the purpose of coaching myself through our challenges.

I'd start feeling fearful or overwhelmed and write about how I knew I should think and how I should feel, and by doing so, I tested the principles in tougher situations than I had EVER faced prior to 2000.

Setback On Top of Setback

We had a rental in California that we were trying to sell to help float the spec homes. One day the realtor went to show the property, and when he turned on the water, the ceiling over the kitchen caved in with a flood of water. The pipes had burst that winter, and nobody had known. We were trying to sell the home, but now it began costing us more money instead.

Anyway, we spent a few thousand fixing the ceiling and the roof, and then our plan was to sell it and roll the profits into a different property with a better positive cash flow.

(That's accomplished by using something called a 1031 exchange - it's a way to defer the taxes until you finally sell your properties and cash out. So long as the proceeds of the home sale goes into another property within a couple months, you don't have to pay income tax on it.)

Well, life was too busy for us to go property shopping. We decided that we needed the profit in cash to keep our business going, even if we would have to pay the income tax.

So we called the 1031 exchange company to say, "Hey, never mind. Go ahead and release the funds because we weren't able to find a property in time."

The recording said, "Our company has filed for bankruptcy. If you want more information, please visit this website." The exchange company had only held our money for six weeks, but now it was completely gone.

When the market crashed and some of our friends began to lose their jobs and face the greatest fears *they've* ever had to face in their lives, I looked back and realized that God allowed me to experience it all, about two years ahead of everyone else. I had been documenting my lessons learned, and I can see how valuable that information was for the millions of people who are now reeling from the effects of this economy. I KNOW I can help, now more than ever. Our hearts told us to take the leap, and although it took time to see the hidden blessings, that decision yielded deeper, more enriching blessings than we ever could have expected.

Choose to Love Your Life. It's a Choice.

When I was in the middle of it, I wasn't ready to be completely candid, because I had to first prove to myself all over again whether or not the principles in *The Jackrabbit Factor* still worked.

I originally thought that what I had discovered and shared through *The Jackrabbit Factor* was the end-all solution to every problem. I didn't see myself ever writing another book, and I could *scarcely* see myself keeping up on a blog.

To be honest, I was bent on creating a service through my book and website that could run itself completely and from which I could disengage and just settle in as the Kool-aid® mom to scrapbook and organize my house.

I since realized that most of my pain and suffering stemmed from wanting to *walk away* from helping others, because every time I got close to the next big financial breakthrough that would allow me to just live in the lap of luxury, it was as if a big rug was once again yanked out from under me.

I felt angry, frustrated, and cynical. I felt like a pawn, knowing that my work was still helping thousands of people achieve their goals, but I couldn't seem to achieve even one more of my own.

Finally, I threw up my hands and said, "Okay, Lord, I guess this is what I do. I am a mom AND a teacher." Period.

Upon deciding to love what I did, I was finally able to say, "Did you know it's a choice? You can love your life or you can choose to hate it. The quicker you find happiness right where you are, the sooner life softens to you again."

Find Happiness NOW - Just as Things Are

That experience reminded me of the time when I moved into the house now posted on my website, www.prosperthefamily.com. I was in the middle of writing *The Jackrabbit Factor*, and I had sold two other homes to afford it. Technically we needed only one of the homes to close escrow, but we didn't want the larger mortgage.

Both homes were in escrow, so we loaded up the U-Haul and headed for Arizona. We parked the truck outside of Grandma's house and spent the night in her basement, expecting the homes to close the next day and get the key to our new house so we could move in.

I was disappointed when it didn't happen the next day. The homes had been in escrow a long time already, so it *truly was* supposed to happen at any moment. After three days I was starting to get a little frustrated. I had six kids cooped up in one bedroom, and most of the things we needed were deeply buried in the U-Haul.

The truck was due to be turned in, and we started racking up late fees. But it would have been ridiculous to unload everything into a storage unit, just to have to rent another truck a day later to move it all out again.

You should have seen me by the end of the week. I was irritable and going stir crazy with nothing to do but wait for the phone call.

By the end of two weeks, I was furious. No longer did I care if both homes closed, I just prayed that ONE of them, either one, would hurry up.

During the THIRD week I wondered if it would fall through altogether. The seller was getting anxious, and we were faced with the prospect of having to start all over.

Finally, out of sheer exhaustion, I collapsed. I cried and cried until I had no more tears, and then decided that it didn't matter any more. I didn't need that house. I would have been thrilled to be in a mobile trailer. All I wanted now was to be in a place of my own that could become our home.

I released my grip on what HAD to be, and found peace *without* it.

Within hours, I got the phone call and was able to move into the house after all. But it didn't happen until I relaxed my grip and found peace without it.

When You Set a Goal, Life Delivers a Challenge

Before long, it became clear that I needed to put together a program that taught the many things I was learning - things that couldn't be effectively shared in just one sitting. What I learned was put into the Family Time and Money Freedom (FTMF) program (www.prosperthefamily.com), with 300 pages of documented lessons learned, for people who need help overcoming financial setbacks.

We've practiced them and seen them continue to work in the face of all of our challenges. Life became our living laboratory to test whether or not they were really true, or whether they were a bunch of *hooey*. I can tell you today that I know they are still true.

As I struggled to create the program, halfway wondering if I was just no longer qualified to teach the principles, deep inside, my heart told me that I was doing exactly what I was supposed to do.

Then life threw one of the toughest lessons my way. *Your disasters, depending on how you respond to them, will either be just a disaster, or they will be a tremendous lesson from which you can profit greatly.*

My question at the time was, "Why does it seem like everything is going wrong? Sure, we're still alive, but is it so wrong to wish for our life to feel abundant again? Should I quit teaching until we figured it out?"

But still, my heart continued to tell me that I needed to teach what I *already knew to be true*, because they were *principles*, and *I wasn't making them true or false by how well I was living them myself.*

About that time, one of my mentors taught me that when you set a goal, life doesn't just deliver the goal. It delivers an experience that, if you respond properly to it, will help you be the person who is capable of receiving the thing you asked for in the first place. The challenge itself is often the very evidence that proves you're on the right track.

The Jackrabbit Factor is not all about getting - it's about becoming. And the more you learn to live by the principles, the more you'll be showered abundantly with everything God has to offer, because you will have learned to respond correctly to the challenges.

Failure is Only Feedback

So, my burning question was whether or not I should just give up.

The experience life delivered to answer that question was this one:

I was in my office when I heard my youngest son yell from downstairs, "Mom! Bethany's lips are blue!" I raced to the backyard where my 7-year-old son had found her 3-year-old little body floating face down in the deep end.

I ran to her side and there was no heartbeat; she was not breathing. I immediately, instinctively threw her over my knee to pat her on the back and dislodge whatever she was choking on - except she, of course, wasn't choking. She had drowned. Do you see how subconscious programs kick in? I goofed up, and it did her no good. So I rolled her over, and her head accidentally hit the deck pretty hard, but there was no complaint. I made another mistake. I tried to give her mouth-to-mouth, but the air only came rushing out of her nose. Another mistake. So I closed her nose and tried again. This time it filled her chest and then stayed there. She didn't naturally expel the air, so it reminded me to press on her chest. A few compressions, another breath, another round of compressions, and she began to revive.

Nobody knows exactly how long she was there, but after an overnight stay in the hospital, she fully recovered.

It wasn't until about 3 weeks later that it finally hit me. God had sent me an answer to my question through this extremely traumatic experience. I could see it clearly. I could see that I had failed time and time again with her - first to keep her safe in the first place, then by making all those mistakes trying to bring her back.

And suddenly I could see our financial situation was in a similar kind of peril. As with our finances, I realized that with every effort to help, I kept making mistakes... but with my daughter, there had been no time to mope or bemoan them. Each mistake actually provided the feedback I needed that helped me ultimately get it right. If I had stopped for even a second to bemoan my mistakes, it could have resulted in her death or long-term handicap.

Because of that experience, I learned that even with our finances, failure is just feedback, and that so long as we have breath to give, there's still time to breathe life into it. If we take too long bemoaning our failures, it can mean death or long-term handicap with our finances, too.

I learned to bounce back quicker from setbacks and stay focused on what we CAN do in the moment. I learned that no matter how bad things may seem, you always have all that you need to do the thing that needs to be done today. It's when you start thinking about what you're going to need next Tuesday that you can get all locked up and useless. Put your blinders on and stay in the moment. If what you need to do in the moment is to avoid problems in the future, then do that by focusing on what you're doing, and not on the disaster you're hoping to avoid.

If you wait until you're perfect before you turn around and help someone else, you'll never help *anyone*.

A final note:

So with all that I've shared with you, and without time to mention all the other mishaps and challenges we've faced, I can stand here and tell you with certainty that the principles of success do still work. The laws of success are still in force, and this economy has become the great sifting ground where we'll find out in a few years who relied on them to get them through, and who caved and decided that the laws are a hoax.

People think that because I'm the Jackrabbit Factor lady, everything is smooth sailing for me. I think it's important for you to know that EVERY new goal stretches me to my limits just as much as the last.

Remember, even when you get what you want, the real prize is who you've BECOME in the process. I'm a different person than I was in 2005, and I wouldn't trade my experiences for anything, because of who I've become and who I'm becoming through the process. Our marriage has endured tremendous stress, and we're stronger for it. Our relationship is deeper than it's ever been in 20 years.

About Leslie Householder
Leslie offers books, audios, videos, home study programs and events that have been proven to help thousands of her clients achieve greater peace of mind in any economy. She shows you how to recognize, enlist, and trust your "gut instinct" for success – the internal guidance system that's already inside of you waiting to be discovered, and which will help you find and follow the fastest, most reliable path to your ideal business and personal life. Life's answers are already inside of

you – she'll help you unveil them. Most of her clients experience their first major transformation in less than 3 hours by reading her flagship story, *The Jackrabbit Factor*, downloadable immediately for free at www.ThoughtsAlive.com.

FINDING YOUR PASSION

Joanne Musa

Humble Beginnings

Ten years ago I was determined to change my financial situation. My husband and I sold our condo in New Jersey, hoping to buy a home for our growing family. We had purchased it in 1989, about 2 weeks after having our first child. A couple of weeks after we moved into our new home, my husband was let go from his job. He was a construction equipment salesman, and we all know what happened to the construction industry in 1990. It was very much then like it is today. He found it very hard to get another job in his industry, so he went to work for himself. I was already self-employed as a personal trainer and had to take time off after having had a C-section.

To say that we struggled financially for a few years would be an understatement. My husband was still in the same industry as a construction equipment broker. The only thing different now was that he worked for himself instead of someone else. We also had no medical insurance, and our income was sporadic. But we still had to pay the monthly bills, so for a while we lived on credit. We did nothing extravagant - didn't go out to dinner, didn't buy little luxuries at the food store or even go out for pizza! We'd cut all of our expenses and went down to one car, but still couldn't make our monthly bills without using credit. We were even using credit cards to pay the mortgage.

When the housing market finally turned around (12 years later) and we were able to sell our condo and actually make a little money instead of owing the bank, we decided to make a move. We both thought that we would be able to find a larger home to rent for awhile (by this time we had three young boys). Our plan was to use some of the money we got from the sale of our home to pay off our debt and improve our credit rating (which had gone in the toilet when we weren't able to pay the bills on time). I also wanted to invest the rest of the money in something that would give us quick profit so that we would have enough money for a down payment on another home in a couple of years.

We were unable to find a suitable house to rent, or anything that we could afford to buy in the county in which we lived. We moved about an hour away to a small 2-bedroom apartment in the town where I had lived as a child. This was 2001, right when the housing market was just starting to take off in the Northeast. For the next four years we looked in three different areas of the state of New Jersey for a home that we could afford to purchase, but were unsuccessful.

Since we couldn't find a home that we could afford in an area in which we wanted to live, we decided to purchase real estate as an investment. The problem with doing that where we lived (and in most of the state at the time) was that rents had not risen at the same rate as the real estate market. We would have to get financing to purchase a property, and the rent that we could collect would not be able to cover the mortgage payments. Still I believed that investing in real estate was the fastest way to build wealth and thus get the money we needed to purchase a home. After reading a lot about real estate investing, I thought that foreclosures or pre-foreclosures might be the answer.

The problem was that the real estate market was booming at this time and investors were paying close to market price for foreclosure homes because the market was rising so fast. At the foreclosure sales that I attended, small distressed houses sold for over $300,000, and that was out of my price range. Also at these sales you needed to have 20 percent of the bid price in certified funds on the day of the sale and the rest within 10 days. Needless to say, I found that we were locked out of the rising real estate market. But we really wanted to get out of our little apartment and into our own home.

How I Became the Tax Lien Lady

I had read something about tax lien investing in Robert Kyosaki's *Rich Dad, Poor Dad* and in Robert Allen's *Multiple Streams on Income*. Neither of these books went into any detail about it. They just mentioned it, but it peaked my curiosity. I picked up the only book in print back in 2001 that was about tax lien investing - *The 16% Solution* by Joel Moskowits. It has since been reprinted, but at the time that I bought it, it was already over 10 years old. (Today, there are plenty of books about tax lien investing in the bookstores and on Amazon, but they are not all written by experts.)

I looked for information online, but it was not easy to find information on tax lien investing back then. I did find one set of e-books which I purchased for less than $25.00, but they didn't give any specific information about how to invest in tax liens. The information in the e-books was very general, gave a description of what tax lien investing was and a lot of hype about what a great investment tax lien certificates are, but not the specific how-to, step-by-step information I was looking for.

Tax lien investing appealed to me because you don't need thousands of dollars to invest like you do with other types of real estate investing. You don't need good credit, and you don't need to negotiate with a buyer or seller. There are no brokerage fees, and you don't have to pay a commission to your financial planner. Your financial planner might not even know anything about tax lien investing.

I did some research to find out more about tax lien investing and started going to tax sales. I met someone else who was trying to do the same thing, only on a much larger scale, so we teamed up to help each other. I found out, when he asked me if I would work for him to purchase tax liens for his portfolio, that he was a multimillionaire with a few successful businesses who was looking for a way to invest his money safely for a higher return than he could get in a money market or CD.

I learned a lot about tax lien investing in New Jersey from working with my new partner. We attended a lot of tax sales and asked the tax collectors questions to find out more about the rules and procedures. I hired a handful of people to help me and trained them on how to do due diligence for tax sale properties and bid at the tax sales. I helped to develop a software program to track the tax lien certificates that we purchased and to automate a lot of the work. During this time my new boss started referring to me as the "tax lien lady." As you'll soon find out, that name stuck.

How Tax Lien Investing Led to My Real Passion (and Livelihood)

Meanwhile, I realized that there were a lot of people out there like me who wanted to learn about tax lien investing, but didn't know where to turn. I started my web site, TaxLienLady.com, to answer questions about how to get started investing in tax liens. I researched tax lien and tax deed investing in every state and wrote a couple of e-books, which I sold through my web site. Then I started doing teleseminars and interviewing experts in different states on aspects of tax lien and tax deed investing. I wrote step-by-step home-study courses on tax lien and tax deed investing, and began doing live seminars for local investing groups.

Now I have multiple home-study courses, web sites, and blogs for tax lien and tax deed investing. I have a tax lien investing podcast on iTunes, Videos on YouTube, and articles on tax lien and tax deed investing that appear all over the internet. I found that my real passion was in teaching new investors about investing in tax liens and tax deeds. My mission is to give people truthful information about tax lien investing, without the hype, and the step-by-step information they need to build a profitable portfolio of tax liens or tax deeds.

My Life Today

Today I am a sought-after expert in the field of tax lien investing, which happens to be an area dominated by men. I didn't let that scare me; somehow I knew it was the right thing to do. I took the same approach to internet marketing, which is also a field that is dominated by men. I don't buy their high-priced programs on "how to make money online," but I do pay attention to what they do. I found successful mentors (who are women, by the way), became their students, and modeled what they did. This allowed me to make money online. I didn't make a lot of money at first, but did cover all of my expenses. Now I'm making what some people would consider a nice income, drive a company car, and am paying two assistants as well.

It's always a little scary when you start something new, and there were times when I wondered if I was doing the right thing. But somehow I knew in my heart that this was the right thing for me, that it would eventually work, and I'd be able to make money at it. With tax lien investing as well as with internet marketing, you don't make money overnight. You have to put time and money in first, and then when your liens redeem or when you've finally built up your reputation and a relationship with your 'list,' the money starts coming in. But you have to be able to tough it out in the early days when you're just getting started.

Faith is what helped me through the early days in my business: faith in myself, faith in God, and faith in others. I also had a lot of support from my family. I may not have been able to start my own business had my husband not had a decent job with good benefits and been very supportive of what I was doing. Finally, the third thing that helped me be successful was the time and money that I devoted to keeping myself motivated. I always spent a portion of the money that I earned (and sometimes even money that I hadn't earned yet) on going to motivational seminars and listening to motivational tapes and CDs. I have gone through different motivational speakers and "coaches." My recent favorite is Tony Robbins. I have attended his live seminars, even taking my husband along with me to one of them.

Nobody Cares as Much about Your Money as You Do

One mistake that I made more than once was in trusting my financial well-being to someone else. As a fitness professional, I excelled at taking charge of my physical well being. I exercised regularly and was very conscious of what I ate. I did not leave my physical well-being up to a physician. I ate right, took supplements, and went regularly to a chiropractor. I had and still have a pro-active attitude about my health. As a result I've been a physically fit individual and a pretty successful athlete, even into my late forties and now in my fifties.

But my fiscal fitness was another story; in fact, I wasn't fiscally fit at all. To be totally honest with you, I'm still working on this area of my life, but I've come a long way. In the past I've trusted my money to others and did not take responsibility for my finances. I left that up to my husband or to a financial planner. I found out early on in our marriage that my husband was worse than I was at handling money. At least I kept my checkbook balanced!

So from the beginning of my married life, I was the one who handled the finances and paid the bills. I was also the one who was stressed out over our financial situation because I knew how bad it was. I resented the fact that the responsibility for handling the money and paying the bills fell solely on me. I wanted someone else to help get us out of the financial mess we were in and tell me what to do with our money.

At first this strategy seemed to be the answer. I consulted with a financial planner who helped us consolidate our debt and get a home equity loan (at 18% interest - remember this was back in the early 90's). At this point we only had a few thousand dollars of credit card debt and a car loan. We were told that this would actually be a savings, because they could write off the interest on the loan and there would only be one payment each month. The only problem was that without a steady income, we couldn't pay the loan on time every month. At first I borrowed the money from credit cards to pay the loan. Later when we were finally in a position to start paying back the debt and I added up what was owed on credit cards, it had ballooned to more than what it had been when we first consolidated the debt into a home equity loan.

This is when I decided that I needed to learn something about money management and take an interest in managing the family finances. I think that the problem is that people wait until they have enough money to manage before they learn how to do it effectively. If you wait until you have what you consider "enough" money to learn how to manage it efficiently, you'll never have enough, because you first have to learn how to manage a little before you're given more.

This was the first turning point for me, even before I knew anything about tax lien investing. It was then I decided to take control of the family finances, instead of blaming my husband for not doing it and looking to "experts" to tell me what to do with my money. I finally decided to learn all that I could about personal finance. I started by reading books and then taking courses, and more importantly acting on the information that I was consuming. This is what eventually led me to tax lien investing and then to internet marketing.

Focus Your Energy

Anything that you want to be really good at takes focused energy. When I was focused on being an athlete, I became the #1 woman master weightlifter in the country. I was also competitive on the national level against women half my age. But when I started coaching and started putting more energy into coaching my son, as he was becoming a top athlete in his age group, I lost my edge as a competitor. Now I was splitting my time and energy between my own training and coaching.

A similar thing happened as my web site became more popular and I started creating more courses to teach people how to invest in tax liens. As I got busy "coaching" others instead of building my own portfolio, I had less time to pay attention to my own investing. In my case, I was just as happy teaching others how to invest and helping them be successful as I was doing it for myself. When one of my students is successful, I get the same thrill that I do when I coach my son to win a national weightlifting competition or get a new personal record.

I also noticed that when I scattered my energy by following the next big thing or whatever bright, shiny object was in front of me, I lost momentum. As long as I focused my energy on tax lien investing, I did pretty well. So I learned to stick with what I know best and to keep working at it until I get the result that I'm after. Success comes from consistent effort at one strategy, and then when you're successful in one area and you've got everything in place, you can move on to another strategy or area and focus your attention on that.

Work on Yourself and the Money Will Follow

Another lesson that I learned was to work on myself first. When I first got disgusted with my financial situation, I read a lot of books about personal finance. The only problem was that just as with the fitness field or any other field, there are as many opinions as to what is the best way to become financially fit as there are opinions on how to become physically fit. Each author has his own strategy, and sometimes it conflicts with the advice of other experts.

The bottom line is that other people's strategies don't always work for you. Real change comes from inside you. I came to realize that it wasn't just outside circumstances that got me into debt in the first place. It was my thinking. We are our thoughts; we become what we think about. We create our own reality with our thoughts and actions. My thoughts and actions had gotten me to where I was financially; it was no one's fault but my own.

Once I realized that I was responsible for my situation, and I had the power to change it, I started reading self-improvement books, not just books about money. The more I improved myself and my own spiritual condition, the better I got at money management, relationships, and just about every other area of life. This is an ongoing journey for me, and I continue to read books on self-help and spiritual development, though not at the same voracious rate I did a few years ago.

Help Yourself by Helping Others

When I first started my web site TaxLienLady.com, I did it to create another stream of income and bring in some extra money. But after a while I found out two things. The first was that I really liked helping people and answering their questions about tax lien investing. The second was that the more I helped others, the more money I was able to earn. When I focused on what I could do to bring in more money, I would work harder and maybe bring in a little more money. But when I focused on my customers and subscribers and what I could do to help them, or how I could better serve them, my income always went up. I think that Zig Ziglar was really on to something when he said, "You can have everything in life you want if you will just help enough other people get what they want."

Success Leaves Clues

"Success leaves clues" is a quote from my favorite success coach, Tony Robbins. Tony has become extremely successful in every area of his life by modeling the most successful people he can find in these areas. This modeling is something that I have adapted in my life as well. I look for mentors in areas of my life in which I want to improve. I became a very successful weightlifter because I had an excellent coach. Now I have an online success coach as well. Sometimes it might be as simple as reading a book by an "expert" in your field, or going to a live seminar or buying a course from someone you respect. I've even created a web site, www.TaxLienLadyRecommends.com where I can recommend my mentors and programs that have helped me, to others.

There is a saying; "When the student is ready, the teacher will appear." Set your intentions, have a clear idea of what you want to do, and the opportunity to learn from the right person will present itself. You just need to recognize it when it comes your way.

Summary

The lessons that I've learned in the last 10 years can be summarized in the following statement: Take responsibility, stay focused, constantly work on improving yourself, help others, and find a good mentor. And just as important are the things that I didn't let get in my way. I didn't worry about the fact that I didn't always know everything I needed to, I just took the next step. You can't always see to the end of the road that you're traveling. You can only see a few yards in front of you at a time. So take the first steps. If you find that you're going in the wrong direction, you can always correct your course. But it's easier to correct your course when you're in motion and actually doing something to get closer to your goal. Somehow you have to find the courage to follow your heart and move ahead, even if you don't know where it will take you or what the next step after that will be.

About Joanne Musa

Joanne works with investors who want to reap the rewards of investing in profitable tax lien certificates and tax deeds. Her tax lien investing articles appear all over the Internet. Her no-nonsense, straightforward approach to tax lien investing has earned her the title of the "Tax Lien Lady." As the owner of Tax Lien Consulting

LLC, she has developed a full line of educational courses for investing in tax lien certificates and tax deeds. You can get her free special report, *7 Steps to Building Your Profitable Tax Lien Portfolio* at www.TaxLienInvestingBasics.com

STEPPING INTO THE UNKNOWN

By Phillip Davis

"I wonder what kind of day it was today?" The thought startled me, like an unexpected gust of wind. I stared up at the clear night sky while my right hand fumbled for the tangled set of car keys. It had been another twelve-hour day at the ad agency, filled with voice mails, emails, client meetings and looming deadlines. *"Did it rain? Was it cloudy? Had it been warm and sunny?"*

I had no idea, no notion, my mind trapped inside a maze of pressing issues that left me reaching for the nearest exit. I opened the door to my Isuzu Trooper, slipped into the driver's seat and sealed myself inside its metallic hull.

It wasn't the first time I was struck hard by a seemingly ordinary thought. A recent encounter with a new acquaintance proved equally unsettling. After exchanging handshakes, I noticed an alert quality in his eyes, a present-mindedness that underscored his availability to the moment. He listened intently, fully engaged in every word I shared. Yet I knew my own mind was racing to the next moment.

"There must be another way to live than this!" I whispered under my breath. On the ride home I felt the hollowness of the day gnawing at my insides. I knew what I would face – a home filled with the same chaos that echoed inside me. The lives of my wife and four children had come to mirror mine, scattered in a myriad of directions, filled with distractions. The fast food wrappers confirmed my suspicions, another day of frenetic activity in the pursuit of more.

"More what?" I questioned. I had achieved everything I wanted to do. I had my own marketing company, new cars, a vacation home, timeshares, and rental properties. I had set goals and met them - notebooks full of them - yet something was missing. I was missing. I wasn't there for my own life – trapped in a perpetual thought bubble of preoccupation and worry. Shortly after that starry night drive home, I spoke with my wife.

"My soul is dying," I told her.

Yes, it sounded dramatic, but I didn't know how else to explain it. There wasn't anything outwardly that I could pinpoint to justify the claim. She knew that my work was stressful at times, and we had talked about making changes in our lives, but suddenly the talk had shifted to action.

"What do you want to do?" she asked, her eyes probing for some hint of direction, some remedy that might resolve the matter.

"I want to move… to the Blue Ridge Mountains," I half-stated, half-blurted.

"Up to North Carolina?" she asked with concern.

"Yes! I just think it would be for the best."

"But what about your business? What about Joe attending charter school?" My wife Michelle and I had discussed eventually retiring to the mountains of western North Carolina, but that would be years later, after making money, saving for retirement, and selling the business.

"I can't wait that long," I said with a new-found certainty. Something had shifted in me, a knowingness that came from a different, yet somehow familiar source. I heard a speaker at a monthly business meeting mention that he had left his position, a tenured college professorship, to sell real estate franchises in another state. He spoke of following an inner path of synchronicity and how that new path revealed itself through tell-tale signs, almost like bread crumbs, confirming the direction. He went on to become a millionaire many times over. To someone like myself, bent on analyzing, predicting and anticipating the future, this type of life navigation seemed fuzzy and haphazard. To think that someone could simply trust life set off every alarm in my mind. My own father, a minister, had died in a tragic motorcycle accident at the age of 38. Trusting an inner, knowing path vs. a detailed, action plan seemed dangerous; yet it held a certain promise, a sense of calm and peace that had evaded my life. Against all reason, and a faith born of love, Michelle agreed to the move – a move to a place where we had no relatives, no friends, and no business connections. It was a move into seeming nothingness, just nature and each other.

Business had not been good. The terrorist attack of 9/11 was recent news, and companies had cut back their advertising in the wake of the disaster. My partner and I had a long-term business plan that did not include me running off to the mountains. My first steps in following my heart, my inner intuition, turned unexpectedly ugly, with disputes about money, property, dividing assets and control of the business. In the end, I left with no business assets but also no business debt.

To make matters worse, I suffered a sudden attack of pancreatitis, which then led to gall bladder surgery. The day of our move, I slipped on a small toy and broke my left foot. This seemed to be anything but the promised path of synchronicity. Undeterred, we forged ahead. After searching dozens of houses, we found a large six-bedroom home nestled on a hilltop overlooking the Blue Ridge Parkway. It had two streams, a pond and woods. It had been on the market a number of months, and we bought the home for less than the appraised value.

Finding a great home was one thing, finding a way to support it was quite another. With a broken foot, no friends, family or local connections, we were living on what little we made off the sale of our rental properties, while paying off large debts. Something significant would have to happen for me to make a living in a town of 8,000, all while working from home. Just before leaving Tampa, my partner suggested I try to sell a web site I had created for some of our auto dealers. The dot com bomb had gone off a couple years before, and the market was not good for selling web sites. Yet after just a couple of calls, I received an offer to buy the site. The new buyers stipulated that they would only buy it if they could make payments. Soon we had a monthly check coming in, enough to pay the mortgage on the house.

Shortly afterwards, my life insurance agent called to check up on me about the recent sickness, surgery and broken foot. He then informed me that since these incidents overlapped, I was entitled to full disability income for an entire year, an added benefit in my policy of which I wasn't even aware. I was suddenly making nearly $10,000 a month, almost entirely tax-free.

Still, I had no long-term means of support. My vision was simply to circle the wagon around my family, live a more tranquil life and find a higher "good" to work towards, something more meaningful than screaming car ads and last minute media buys. With my temporary financial freedom, I was able to sit by my pond, ponder, read and heal.

The more I read, (and I read lots), the more I realized there was no ultimate "good" to "do." My whole life had consisted of doing, and doing had never proved fulfilling. It was an "if-then" mentality that kept the chase in place, doing more, wanting more, reaching for more. It was as if the universe was sending a not so subtle message that the ultimate "good" was to simply be. I began to relax just a little. And I began to trust.

In the weeks that followed, with time on my hands, I started a web site devoted to what I truly love to do – creating environments where people thrive. It took the form of a branding agency, a company that could help business owners better define and communicate who they are and what they do. It was my own search for congruency, clarity and alignment that lead to the name Tungsten Branding, based on the filament in the light bulb. Tungsten is one of the densest metals known to man and glows brightly only because it is so resistant. In many ways I could relate to this little wire in the bulb. I had wrestled and resisted so much in life that I felt burnt out, and now a new energy was beginning to flow through me, one that radiated on its own. Naturally. Effortlessly.

From this simple beginning, I added content to the site, began to write articles for sites such as IdeaMarketers.com, blogged on what I knew and ran a small Google Adwords campaign. In a matter of weeks, I had my first few clients. They ranged from start-ups to international firms. Within months I had projects from Malaysia and Hong Kong to Australia and India.

What I was told could not be done in the Tampa Bay market (branding firms are typically located in cities such as New York and San Francisco with lots of corporate headquarters) I was now doing in Brevard, North Carolina. In the past eight years the business grew from a home office to a loft on Main Street. Along with branding projects came opportunities to consult, speak and travel. In the past eight years Tungsten Branding has named over 200 companies, products and services. But the benefits stretched beyond the business.

Our family also became ingrained in the fabric of this small, tight knit community nestled in the mountains. We helped start the town's annual White Squirrel Festival, the biggest retail event of the year, attracting 25,000 visitors each Memorial Day weekend. The youngest of our crew joined scouting with trips to Camp Daniel Boone. We hiked the many trails of the Blue Ridge Mountains, tubed down Davidson River and camped at the local lake. All four kids participated in some form of music and band. We had friends visit several times a year to enjoy the seasons. Most importantly, I began to notice what type of day it was. This was a different type of success, not based on numbers, but on the ability to connect. My navigational system shifted from "thinking it out," to following a deeper, more intuitive path.

The Lessons Learned

I say "the lessons learned" with an inner smile, since I've come to realize these lessons are never fully learned, just reinforced again and again. I still have days where I'm wrapped up in thought, worry about inconsequential issues and have to be asked a question twice. The teenagers roll their eyes at me, and complain there's not enough "to do" in our little community. But it's all wonderfully normal stuff.

This book title starts with "trust your heart" because that's where it all begins – the ability to tune into that still small voice, the one that gets drowned out by every other noise in life. But if we are to look at lessons, here are some worth noting.

1. There's more than one way to navigate life.

Most of our lives we struggle with this battle between our hearts and our heads. The mind is an awesome tool when guided by something other than self-promotion and advancement. So let your mind do all the hard work and rowing it wants, but let your heart do the steering. And when I say heart, I mean that feeling that comes from our gut, the one that gives us the all-clear sign or the "no go" sign. We all know the feeling, but it takes awareness to quiet the noisy brain and allow the heart to be heard. Some people refer to it as a sense of "knowingness," a wisdom that comes from somewhere beyond the limited confines of our own life experience.

2. Pain can sometimes be your friend.

Like most of these lessons, this is one I learned the hard way, but it comes with a silver lining. It's also what prompted my journey. I had reached a point where I felt miserable, stuck and unhappy, but nothing changed until I was in enough pain to do something about it. I often run into people now, both personally and professionally, who are in some "stuck" situation. They want a change; they want to do something different; they don't like the way things are now in their lives, but they just can't do anything about it. When they ask for my advice, I often tell them to pray for more pain. Shocked, they often pull back as if I hadn't heard right or misunderstood their concern. But I reassure them that I heard exactly what they said and that I can relate.

They have the worst of both worlds, a problem and no solution. If someone is sick, but not sick enough to go to the doctor, he/she will just suffer. If someone is holding onto an electric fence and getting shocked, but not enough to let it go, then someone needs to up the voltage. If you have a dream in your heart and keep finding ways to avoid taking the steps, ask if you've had enough pain yet. Pain is the gift to our bodies to take action, and it's the gift to our lives to make a shift.

3. You will feel fear, and it's just an emotion.

If pain is the "gas" to get us moving forward, fear is the "brake" that holds us back. A great way to deal with fear is to ask yourself what you would do right now, if your success was 100% guaranteed. In other words, if you could not possibly fail, what would you do? That usually sets the gears in motion. "I would do this, then that, then I would do this, etc." It typically starts to flow right out. So the real issue is not "what do I do," or "how to do it," but simply fear itself. And fear is just an emotion.

Watch the fear like you watch a storm cloud. It blows in and rumbles and makes noise, and then it goes. The beauty of living your dream is that you really only need to deal with the present moment, the present issue. But when looking ahead in fear, you are dealing with innumerable fears all at once. And as Mark Twain once said, *"I've suffered* a great *many* catastrophes in my life. *Most* of them *never* happened."

4. Things won't turn out as you plan, (but they might turn out better).

I have a very wise friend who once shared that he prefers not to over-plan things. When I asked him why he felt this way, he offered this explanation. "When you plan everything out, you might get what you want, but you'll also miss out on what you could have had." It's very similar to a vacation trip, where the end destination becomes so important that nothing gets noticed along the way. In much the same manner, as you go for your dream, hold the intention in place - the end destination - but be open to how you might get there. You may find yourself "rerouted" at times. And the new route might prove more interesting, more challenging and more rewarding than what you had envisioned in your own mind.

5. Keep your real goal in mind at all times.

This ties back to the previous lesson. Let's say your goal is to make $80,000/ year from home. Make sure this is your real goal before you start your journey. A good way to test your goals is to ask the question, "So I can what?" Let's try an example.

- Beginning Goal: "I want to make $80,000 a year from home."
- Question: So you can what?
- "So I won't have to commute so far to and from work."
- Question: So you can what?
- "So I can spend more time with my husband and family."
- Question: So you can what?
- "So I can feel more connected and close to those I love."
- Question: So you can what?
- "So I will feel less guilty and more present minded."
- Question: So you can what?
- "So I can relax and begin to enjoy my life."

- Question: So you can what?
- "So I can be at peace."
- Real goal: To be at peace

The reason I bring this up is that you may find that you don't need $80,000/year from a stay-at-home job to find a sense of peace and present mindedness. You might start that direction and find an opportunity that pays half that amount, but the work proves rewarding, and you come home refreshed and energized. If you remain fixed on the first scenario, you could end up as a day trader, shut in a back room, trying to get to your goal of $80,000, when in fact you simply want to connect with your loved ones. I make less now than I did in some of my biggest earning years, but have a life immersed in family and friends and surroundings that keep me centered and grounded. By digging down and discovering your true goal, you can allow new opportunities to emerge without being threatened. Instead of fighting to get to a predetermined goal, you can now embrace new paths that will take you to what you really want. As in the example above, you could experience life more deeply and be at peace.

Trusting your heart is a process that begins with courage. The path may seem uncertain at first, but in reality life is always uncertain, whether we acknowledge this fact or not. It's the illusion that we can control and manipulate our lives that keeps us holding tight to what we have, planning and predicting, rather than experiencing and enjoying. It's a different way to navigate life, one that relies upon a deeper source of wisdom than the conflicting motives of the mind. By placing an intention in your heart and watching it unfold, you become witness to the mystery of what life has to offer. You are then free to create and recreate. And in those present minded moments, you won't have to wonder what kind of day it was – you'll be fully living it.

About Phillip Davis

Phil is the owner and president of Tungsten Branding (www.PureTungsten.com), an identity firm specializing in brand creation, alignment and strategic positioning. Phil has more than 20 years of company branding and marketing experience, having personally named over 200 regional, national and international businesses, products and services. While the size of the companies may vary, the branding issues are frequently similar in nature… the need for better clarity, direction and vision. Phil's own firm, Tungsten Branding, is a reflection of this conviction. His goal of creating brilliance and clarity is demonstrated in both his work and his commitment to help his clients achieve brand excellence.

Phil has penned over fifty articles on naming and branding, as well as speaking on the subject to numerous business and industry trade groups nationwide. He has written for, or been quoted in, Inc.com, Entrepreneur.com, AOL Small Business, Business Week, and TV Guide, as well as a variety of national trade publications. He has helped to brand everything from municipalities to book titles to the town's annual White Squirrel Festival.

When not naming and branding, Phil resides with his wife, four kids and three dogs in the Blue Ridge Mountains of Western North Carolina.

It's All About Relationships

Lisa Rae Preston

From teaching children how to read to filming classroom plays to nourishing the dreams of innocent hearts, I'd taught kindergarten through fourth grades for fourteen years and overall felt completely fulfilled in life. My work, though, was becoming increasingly stressful as our school system began to concentrate on upping test scores no matter what the cost. The very creativity and life seemed zapped right out of the classroom as we were forced to "practice" for the end of the year test 2-3 hours a week.

I began to face "burn out." By my seventeenth year, I was teaching half-time and looking online for possible ways to make money. The growing stress of politics in teaching negatively affected my health, and after the half-time year, I did what I never dreamed possible – turned in my resignation papers.

I surely don't recommend quitting one job before you have another one in tow, but I didn't feel as if I could survive the stress of the old one any longer.

My precious grandmother encouraged me every step of the way. I wasn't sure how to make money online and was for all practical purposes, a pre-embryonic newbie when it came to using the computer.

All I had done with the bulky Mac I shared with the teacher next door was type a science test and print it out. But still, I felt drawn to learning how to set up my own online business.

Since I had researched accelerated learning techniques and neuroscience for many years, I decided it made sense to set up a homeschooling website on how to learn faster and easier. Creating a website proved to be one of the most trying obstacles I had ever faced. Just when it seemed I was getting a grasp on technology, there'd be another piece of software to learn, and quite frankly, I hardly knew how to install software.

Relentlessly, I moved forward, reading technical manuals and plowing through marketing courses.

After a year online, I had made a whopping $94. My investment had been nearly $7000. This was not a good sign. I tried selling wholesale on e-Bay, only to find two thirds of my house stocked with liquidations no one wanted.

Oops.

I tried affiliate marketing, joint venture brokering, virtual assisting, niche marketing with fancy software, and creating my own products. By this time my income had increased to around $700 total. Unfortunately, my expenditures on coaching and "the next best products" ran around $20,000.

The first breakthrough of insight for me came when I attended one of my grandmother's rehab appointments with an occupational therapist. At the age of 89, Gran had experienced a stroke and faced learning to walk and to speak again. Thankfully, since I was no longer teaching, I could help take care of her.

At this particular session, I watched as the therapist took Gran's hands in her own and gazed at her with pride and encouragement. Gran threw back her head and laughed, a newfound confidence declaring, "I'm going to conquer this!"

Even though I sat right beside my grandmother, our arms touching - it seemed as if I floated above the whole scene. The smile of the therapist mixed with the laughter and joy of my most precious grandmother seemed to take on a life of its own. It was as if I was watching a *tangible transfer of hope from one heart to another.* I felt profoundly affected for days afterward, reflective and realizing with intensity that the moment I'd witnessed was a part of my destiny and would change the rest of my life.

In one forgettable epiphany, I understood that the kind of connection I'd witnessed – that tangible transfer of hope – was what I was to be about online. In a place where people increasingly feel invisible and almost more of a number than a human being, cyberspace thrived on automation, not heart-to-heart connection.

I felt that part of my mission was to reach through the computer screen, grasp hands with the person on the other side and somehow impart hope. How to personalize the internet like that – I had no idea. But I felt it was possible and that I'd find a way.

Fast forward two and a half years. I'd tried multiple ways to make money online, including a 6-month coaching stint with a well-known marketer. My first product didn't even make it to the point of being sold. My second product did a bit better, but still only sold around 67 copies. Little by little I'd experienced brief episodes of success, but nothing long-lasting.

My grandmother was supporting me on her $647 a month social security check, and I had a little savings left. We were in this together, and I wanted to succeed for her as much as for myself. No matter what frustrations I faced, Gran continued to cheer me on at every turn. She felt deeply that I could achieve my dream and encouraged me to persevere.

I began attending internet marketing seminars to meet other marketers and learn the ropes. At one conference I was invited to a mastermind group with highly successful entrepreneurs. The meeting shocked me. These master marketers were sharing the frustrations of moving from a six-figure income to beyond, and I felt like a kindergartener in a college classroom. That night I sobbed myself to sleep, wondering what I was doing in this crowd who knew so much more than I did. How on earth could I ever be successful?

My dream of making money online hung on by a thread.

During the next seven weeks I came up with numerous ideas for products, but none that seemed to really connect with me. One evening I sat in my living room, desperate to brainstorm that winner product. I wrote a list of the strengths I brought to the table. What did I do well that could be of service to other marketers?

Write emails! Numerous subscribers on my email list had written me saying they felt like I was conversing with each of them one-on-one, even though they knew that I was writing to thousands at once. "I love reading your emails!" they'd say.

So I could compose a relationship building email message. And writing follow-up emails definitely seemed to be a challenge and frustration for many marketers.

But was there a way I could make creating email marketing messages easier for them? My brain went wild. Simple templates could never capture the personality of the marketer, so templates were out of the question. Could I create a piece of software for website owners that would write a year's worth of follow-up emails in any niche, all personal and relational - emails that created trust and encouraged subscribers to buy from the site?

Sounded like science fiction, but I couldn't let go of the idea. I ran it past a couple marketing friends who encouraged me, "If you can make it work, you'll have an instant hit on your hands."

Of course, my mind was swirling with a tug of war. "How on earth can a piece of software be created that takes on the personality of its user?"

I had already burned bridges by not renewing my teaching certificate. It was succeed or go down with the ship. My grandmother kept encouraging me. "Lisa Rae," she'd say, "I am proud of you, and I know you can do anything you set your mind to. Don't give up!"

I kept brainstorming. At this point, the potential software took on a new look. It wasn't just about making money – it was about helping marketers create relationship-building emails and to build trust online. Customers are not just numbers - there's a real person with a real heart behind each order. Perhaps this software creation was part of a way to reach through cyberspace and actually connect hands with others.

The problem came in seeking to in some way "automate relationship" so that the process was less time consuming, but still genuine. How could relationship building be automated?

Another obstacle was that I didn't know much about computers and certainly had never had training in developing software. I did have a software "kit" that could help you make simple software without having to learn coding. But even that was difficult for me to comprehend. I kept at it hours every day and thankfully had some assistance from a friend who knew the software kit inside out. She graciously helped me whenever I ran into issues, which was often!

Fortunately, I had no idea until after the fact that others had tried to create a similar software for years and had not succeeded. Ignorance was bliss. I walked around in complete brain turmoil for two days trying to figure out how to put the pieces together to make it all work.

During those two days, I must have tried a hundred different ways to create the core pattern for the software. It involved constantly throwing away ideas and going back to the drawing board.

Finally the eureka moment sparked my brain into action. Software users would put in 3-4 hours of research and then insert that information into the software. Then with the click of a button, 52 personality-filled, follow-up marketing emails would be ready to go.

Two months after the initial idea, the site was launched. It took 8 weeks of non-stop work. And it paid off!

Instant Niche Emails proved to be an instant bestseller with niche marketers. Every few hours, I'd run to Gran's house and give her an update. "We're at $30,000, Granny!" And she'd kick up her heels from her chair and yell, "Hallelujah! I knew you could do it!" It seemed as if we had accomplished the work together.

At the $50,000 mark, I convinced Gran to let me buy new carpet for her house. She'd needed new carpet for years, but couldn't afford the investment.

"Now, Lisa Rae, I don't want you to go spending your money on me," she insisted. But I brought the carpet samples over anyway and told her the installers were coming. She finally gave in and chose a speckled Berber sample. Words couldn't capture my joy! Finally, I could give back to my wonderful cheerleader and best friend.

The date was set. December 13 the carpet guys were coming over – just two weeks away. Gran had complained about that carpet for years, and I knew she'd be thrilled with the new look.

A couple days later I received a call from Granny, and she could only speak in garbles. I drove to her house in a panic. We found out later she'd had an allergic reaction to a medication.

Nine days later, my dearest friend who shared my very heartbeat, passed away.

My voice broke as I called the carpet shop and cancelled our appointment.

Over the next months, I fell into a deep depression, hardly able to get out of the bed some days. Thankfully, the software continued to sell well, despite my hiatus. The days seemed to grow darker and darker, and I sought counseling from more than one person. I could barely think.

Eventually, the business which I had built dwindled. It was a long, difficult road back. Many days I wanted to throw in the towel. Over the past five years, though, I've learned some of the greatest lessons of my life, including a strong passion and calling in life - creating healing programs for those who have been deeply traumatized.

Today I am able to move ahead in different ways. I am stronger and more resilient. I have healthier boundaries and a deeper ability to share from my heart. The lessons I learned along the way have been priceless, as have been the relationships built.

Life keeps taking on new meaning at every turn, and I am inspired to continue reaching out online, grasping hands with my readers, and I trust, imparting a sense of hope.

Lessons I Am Learning Along the Way

Lesson #1 Choose to Connect with Your Customers

Be passionate about connecting with subscribers and customers. Showing that you're a real person, not just a "faceless" company is imperative in any kind of marketing and especially in any kind of online business. Nurturing the subscribers and clients you have is crucial if you want to continue to grow.

You can build relationship in a variety of ways. For instance, if someone trusts you enough to purchase your product, send a personal thank you email, and if it's a really high-ticket item, pick up the phone and connect with the person. The impact you make will set you apart from any competitor.

Another way to connect with your website visitors is to write in a way that touches their hearts. You've likely heard the quote, "People will forget what you've said, they'll forget what you've done, but they'll never forget how you made them feel."

Touch your readers' emotions in a way that helps them feel stronger for having read your material. How does your product, salesletter, webpage, newsletter make your reader *feel*?

Every part of your site and every step of the way, personalize as much of your marketing as possible. Connect, connect, connect.

Lesson #2 Develop a Thick Skin

Sometimes you'll get a negative response, no matter how hard you try to help people. Grow in character to embrace criticism in business without being shaken by it in your heart. This suggestion is a lot easier said than done!

You just never know what people are experiencing. Perhaps that agitated woman's only son was killed in an auto accident last month. Maybe the mean-mouthed man received the news – "malignant" instead of "benign." The customer could be so stressed out, she doesn't know where to turn.

I once received an email from a lady who was ticked off that I had launched a new product for $297. She vented. How dare I act like I cared about people who were just starting out and charge more than they could afford! I should be giving more away, not demanding money. The rant went on and on.

Well, I wrote back with an explanation of how much work went into the product and how much work we were doing with each client. Then I just prayed a blessing over her – for increased finances and joy.

She wrote back and said that my response had made her cry. She was a single mom in the middle of an illness and trying to take care of her children. She wasn't sure some days how she would make it.

So we don't know someone else's circumstances. It's not always easy, but make every effort to respond to a customer with gentleness and honor.

Lesson #3 Take responsibility for your own business by developing a strong marketing mindset.

Part of taking responsibility for your business includes marketing regularly, day in and day out. Marketing really is a numbers game. The more people with whom you share your message, the more sales you are likely to make. Plus, having a long list of potential clients takes a lot of stress off your mind. If one person says no, it's not a big deal. You still have dozens more possibilities!

Marketing requires a continual forward motion. That's not always easy for the creative entrepreneur who loves to write new products! The key here is to reframe the marketing so that you can be inspired by the process. That will keep the creative genius from becoming a starving artist!

The numbers game proves true for partnerships, too. If you want to find partners to help sell your products, scout for dozens of potential associates! Then if one or even twenty of them say no, it's no sweat off your brow. You still have many more possibilities.

Also, don't get in a situation where you're desperately depending on a certain deal to go through with another person. Businesses can switch gears in a heartbeat, and if you've been calculating all the profits you and a partner will make together and in the process abandoned some of your own work, you end up on the losing end. Plus, the relationship can end up extremely strained or ruined.

Always focus on your business first. At the end of the day, it's you - the business owner - who writes your own paycheck. Never calculate the "money you're likely to make" as real money. It's not cashable until it's deposited in your bank account.

Some of the best advice I've gotten in regard to entrepreneurship? Don't wait for others to act. Be a mover and a shaker yourself.

Lesson #4 Build Connections.

With the endless amount of new information necessary to maintain an online business, it's crucial to interact with others who can help you accomplish the tasks you don't know how to do yet and who've "been there-done that" and know the shortcuts.

1. Seek out business partners with whom you really resonate. At first, it may not be easy to find folks who have the same values and heart as you do, but keep searching. Connecting with like-minded individuals makes business more joyous.

2. Get everything in writing when partnering with someone – because it's too easy to forget what was said in a conversation and too easy to presume you're both on the same page. I love the way one of my friends puts it - "I'm not asking for this in writing because I don't trust you. I wouldn't be doing business with you if I didn't trust you. I want us to be completely clear on what we're saying so that it's truly a win/win for both parties."

   Clarifying all the details on paper is one of most intelligent and honoring decisions you can make in a partnership.

3. Seriously consider hiring a coach to help you stay on task and move you toward success. If there was only one thing I could choose to do over from the beginning, it would be to have hired a coach right off the bat. Coaching may seem expensive, but it can save you lots of money in the long run, as you're learning what really works and not investing in products that won't fit your needs.

Lesson #5 It's okay to market your product.

I have spent too much time agonizing over the idea of selling stuff to people! Deep down, my belief was that salesmen take advantage of others. Since I wanted to be a person of integrity, I had a hard time doing the marketing end of things.

The remedy for this struggle is easy. First off, be sure you're marketing a solid product of which you can be proud. Write down all the benefits of the product and consider the number of ways it can help others. If you are selling something that will be blessing to another's life, you are helping them.

If I had to wake up every day thinking, "Oh, how much can I sell today?" I'd quit in a nanosecond. When I get discouraged, chances are I've lost focus that I am here to be a blessing to others. When I wake up thinking, "How many folks can I help today realize their destinies?" then I'm on a roll and fired up and experience much greater motivation and success.

Remind yourself from time to time what your business is really all about and why you're in it.

If your website visitors buy your product, they'll be blessed. If not, then perhaps you can just be an encouragement to them through your newsletter. It's all about reaching out, connecting and blessing.

About Lisa Rae Preston
Lisa Rae Preston, ex-school teacher turned online entrepreneur, is the author of bestselling software Instant Niche Emails and the STEP into Destiny Passion Test as well as numerous other niche info-products. Known best as a 'Relationship Marketer', Lisa focuses on helping others establish a trusting connection online with their clients and potential customers.

Lisa Rae's background in personality theory and neuroscience research gives her a unique perspective on creating and maintaining thriving client relationships. She focuses on the personality of each niche market with which she works, and specializes in building trusting relationships amid the "uncertainty and skepticism" of cyberspace.

Lisa Rae now keeps busy speaking, writing, and coaching clients in building businesses around their passions. You can find out more about her program Instant Niche Emails at www.InstantNicheEmails.com and take the STEP into Destiny Passion test at www.StepIntoDestiny.com.

How I Turned $194 Into Millions by Following My Heart

Adam Urbanski

How a train trip to Vienna, a ripped up plane ticket, and a short Facebook post helped me discover seven lessons that can make your dreams come true!

> *"The most difficult thing is the decision to act, the rest is merely tenacity."* - Amelia Earhart

Most people who know me are familiar with my story of coming to the United States with only $194 in my pocket, just a high-school education, starting out without speaking English and with no connections, and turning my efforts into a multi-million dollar success in only 10 years.

But until now, I have never shared the story of how I got to come to the United States in the first place.

You see, deep inside I always knew that I wanted to live in America. So when I turned 18 and finished high-school, I got serious about making my dream a reality. But thinking about something and actually doing it are two different things. And if you know anything about communist Poland of late 1980's, you may have an idea how my dream was, well… more of a dream than even a remote possibility.

First, you needed a passport. But, unlike in the United States, the government only issued one for specific trips, and it had to be returned to proper authorities after returning to Poland. Since men my age were subject to a mandatory three-year military service and were likely to leave the country to never return, I was told not to even bother applying for a passport until after my military service.

Second, you needed an entry visa to the USA. That required months of standing in line just to get inside the American Embassy. Even then, only one in hundreds of people were granted that amazing stamp in their passport.

Frankly, I only learned many of those things much later, which I guess is a good thing. Because had I known about all the barriers and difficulties I was likely to face, I might have never bothered trying. This is a great lesson in itself, that **if you just start taking action (and don't dwell on all the things that might get in your way or go wrong), you just might end up accomplishing something others think is impossible to do!**

But back to my story…

I heard that it was much easier to actually go to Canada first, then move from Canada to the States. I also heard that it was much easier to get the Canadian visa by applying for it at an embassy in Vienna, Austria instead of Warsaw, Poland. I decided to do just that.

I got my passport for the trip to Vienna. Bought my one-way train ticket. Packed my backpack, said good-bye to friends, siblings, and my teary-eyed mother and stern-faced dad… and got on the train with the intention of never returning. (Well, at least not for a few years!)

The train ride to Vienna was only a few hours. Once there, I headed straight from the train station to the Canadian Embassy. I was shocked that I was able to get right in. I was given an appointment time and told to come back for my visa application interview a few hours later.

With nothing else to do, and with planning on getting my visa then heading straight to the airport to get my plane ticket to fly to Canada, (don't laugh, I really thought it would be that easy), I didn't think of anything to do but to park myself on a bench at a nearby park. I pulled out a sandwich and a book and thought the time would pass quickly. It did, in fact, pass too quickly!

Unknowingly to me, my watch malfunctioned! For some reason, it was stopping every few minutes, then starting again and stopping. You get the picture. So when the watch showed the time I was supposed to be back at the embassy – it was actually over an hour later.

It was a disaster. Without speaking German, I couldn't explain why I was late. I did finally get to see one of the consuls, but after just moments of very animated storytelling, using hand gestures and speaking slower in Polish, (like that's supposed to magically make people who don't speak it understand it!) in no time at all I got my passport stamped – but instead of a visa, it was a big red word "DENIED."

It was now dark outside, and I was totally unprepared for this outcome. Without speaking German… overwhelmed by the big city… with no connections… I got scared! How was I supposed to make it work? Where was I supposed to sleep tonight? Who could I ask for help? The more I thought about all those "scary" things, the more I was overwhelmed by fear and paralyzed into total inaction.

Finally, I pulled out my city map and began walking back to the train station.

On the late night train back to Poland, I felt defeated. Playing in my head what to tell my friends and how to explain this to my family, I realized that I needed a better plan. But more than anything else, I realized that if I really wanted to move to America, **if I really wanted to make my dreams a reality, I needed to be a whole lot more committed.**

It took me a couple of months to shake off the feeling of failure. And I started thinking again how I could get myself to America. It just seemed so impossible to achieve!

Let me quickly paint a picture of how tough it was to get a US visa. I told you earlier that it took months of standing in line to just get inside the embassy building. Then, the odds of actually getting the visa were like winning a lottery.

 Poles were used to standing in long lines for days just to buy meat, sugar, flour, and other basic necessities. But the line to get inside the embassy was ridiculous! Since it was a months-long process, people waiting in line actually formed a "line association," which kept a list of names of everyone and their specific place in line. You had to check in with them every so often, or you'd lose your spot.

I knew I couldn't wait for months, because I was about to be drafted into the military. I had weeks at best before my passport would be taken away, and I would be serving three years in the Polish army – something my entrepreneurial, authority-defying spirit just couldn't take! So I decided to investigate things myself. Despite hearing all those horrific embassy-line stories, I imagined that being the witty and charming young man I was, maybe I could somehow talk my way into the embassy.

Early morning on November 23, 1989, I embarked on a train to Warsaw and around 9 a.m. arrived at the embassy building. I was surprised there were only a few people there (not hundreds that were supposed to be, forming a line curving around several blocks.) Plus, there was a lot of excitement between folks – apparently the embassy was letting people in today, but it was supposed to close its doors early. "Duh," I thought to myself, "of course they are letting people in. Isn't that what they do every day?"

You see, back then I never heard of "Thanksgiving" and had no idea how huge of a holiday it was for the Americans. And, you guessed it – it was a Thanksgiving Day! The embassy was actually supposed to be closed, and that's why most people who had been in line for months didn't bother to show up that day.

A couple of hours later – I WAS INSIDE! This is where it got really interesting!

Remember, I had no clue how this entire process worked! I just showed up for the first time that morning. But people around me had been standing in that line for months. They had complete information on everything happening inside, including the most important thing - which of the consuls was most likely to actually grant a US entry visa.

There was one consul, a woman in her forties, who was rumored to never have issued any visas. It was considered bad luck to be called to her desk. Standing in the waiting room, I could see people haggling with each other when it was their turn and the available consul was that woman.

Finally, I was first in line. I was so nervous. I knew the next few minutes would change my entire life. So many thoughts were rushing through my head. But I was just taking deep breaths and telling myself that I just had to be present, pay attention, and be myself and present myself in the best way I could. And that had to be good enough – because that's all I really could do.

A quick side note. If you've ever been to one of my seminars or seen one of my presentations somewhere, you might have seen a slide of me from those days. If you haven't, imagine this - a long-haired skinny kid, dressed all in black (including an ankle-length trench coat) with so many scarves, it looked as if his head wasn't attached to his body, but was popping out of some sort of wool nest. OK, you get the picture, right? To say the least, it was probably not the type of look that would make you want to spontaneously start a conversation with me.

So, I was the first person in line. And guess who the next available consul was? Yep, that "monster" of a woman, that infamous "queen of the DENIED stamp!" I was hoping to pass my place in line and let the person behind me go first, but NOBODY WAS THAT STUPID! Well, I took a deep breath and stepped forward.

I thought for sure this was where my journey would end. And then it got even worse! You see, the typical interview had to do with proving that you had enough assets in Poland that you would never want to go to America and stay there. So I was armed with bank statements, papers showing I owned a business, and lots of other documentation that I could think of and brought with me to make my case. I was so ready, but instead, she asked me "WHY" I wanted to go to America.

I thought it to be a stupid question. I mean, come on! Had this woman been outside of the embassy building? I thought to myself, "Hello! There are no opportunities here! Hello! I'm being drafted into a mandatory three-year military service! Hello! If you want to buy a kilogram of the crappiest meat or a half a kilogram of sugar, you have stand in line for freaking hours, if not days. Hello! In America you can make in an hour what people in Poland make in 10 freaking years!" I instantly questioned that woman's intelligence! Still, I had to answer her question.

So I decided to just tell her the truth! I said, "From everything I can hear and read, America is an amazing country. I watch the movies and can't even imagine how amazing New York must really be if it looks so great on TV. AND, people say that in America money grows on trees. AND, that Americans are the most friendly people in the world." I made the big gesture pointing to all the people behind me and continued, "That's why we all want to go. That's WHY I want go - to see for myself if all of this is true. And I don't want to wait until I get old like all these people." I pointed behind me.

I remember that for some reason I wasn't nervous at all, once I started talking. I couldn't stop smiling as I was getting all animated with my story. I remember she was piercing me with her eyes, but she was grinning from ear to ear watching me. In her broken Polish she asked me a few more questions, which I can't remember now (I think they had to do with how I was going to pay for my travel expenses or something like that.) Then she took my passport and told me to come back in a couple of hours. I had no clue what that meant and thought I was in trouble.

When I stepped back into the waiting room, I was instantly surrounded by folks wanting to know what mood the consul was in, what questions she asked me and what happened. When I told them I was worried because she kept my passport, they all looked at me like my head wasn't just popping out of a wool nest, but like I had at least two heads!

Finally, someone in the crowd said, "Son, you got your visa!"

Three and a half weeks later, on December 19, 1989, just one day after arriving in New York, I was sitting in my hotel room which was pre-paid for 10 days. I had a suitcase filled with clothes, and my entire financial fortune - $194 – was in my pocket. In my hand I held my non-refundable plane ticket back to Poland. I knew from experience that I needed to commit to my success before getting scared, overwhelmed and paralyzed by fear, and I knew exactly what I had to do.

That plane ticket was my "alternative option" in case I couldn't make things work in America. And at that moment, I knew that if things were to be, it was up to me - that if I really wanted something in life, I had to give it my all, and there could be no "alternative options." A few seconds later, I ripped my ticket in half! Now it was really only up to me!

Now, in case you got lost in my story, I don't want you to lose the lessons I learned from it. Let me recap for you a few of the ideas hidden here that have so profoundly impacted my life and allowed me to reach the success I enjoy today.

1) **Always focus on your dreams**, no matter how unreal they seem or how insurmountable the obstacles stopping you from achieving

them appear to be. The odds against me actually coming to America were stacked so high, nobody around me could see past them. Frankly, neither could I.

But there was a huge blessing in my ignorance. I didn't see the obstacles at all! I just kept thinking about what I really wanted and how it would feel once I had it! And that was the fuel that kept me taking some of the boldest moves!

2) **Take action fast!** The more you think about something, the more likely you are to notice everything that could go wrong. And the more you focus on things that could go wrong, the more likely you are to either not get started at all or actually get the results of which you were most afraid.

Today I teach my clients that if something is worth doing, it's worth doing poorly to start with. It doesn't mean not doing your research or moving forward despite obvious dangers. It simply serves as a reminder that in life things rarely are "completely ready," and they never will be until we take the first step! Then, often as if by magic, when we fully commit and start moving toward our goals, all sorts of "amazing coincidences" occur to aid us in our journey.

3) **Put yourself in a place where you are most likely to succeed.** There is an old saying, "Wherever you go, there you are." But no one ever teaches us that if where you are you can't be WHO you are – and more importantly – who you want to be, you must go elsewhere.

The environment we are in and the people we hang out with have the most significant influence over us. Often, it's a "holding" power that keeps us stuck for years. Perhaps your move doesn't have to be as dramatic as mine, but if your current environment holds you back – change it! Be it an uninspiring room décor or people who never believe in you enough, if you really want to grow, you must move!

4) **Sometimes the simplest course of action is the best!** This lesson escaped me for years. You see, we often perceive things to be difficult or impossible, so we try to figure out ways to go around the perceived problems and thus unnecessarily complicate things – like my "side-tour" to Vienna to get a Canadian visa instead of just going straight to the American embassy.

A good friend of mine taught me a simple mantra: "Oh, what the heck? Let me go for it anyway!" Try it. Go for the most improbable and perceivably impossible idea. You just never know when the Universe will "conspire" to help you out and simply "open the door" when you thought you would never find the key or "build the bridge" when you thought you had to take the detour!

5) **Passionately share your convictions with others.** This lesson also took me years to figure out, but I'm glad I did – because it's more important today than ever before. I believe the "queen of the denied stamp" rewarded me with the visa because I didn't try to come up with some crappy story. Instead, I just said what I meant. Thinking about it, all those years later, I'm convinced she was entertained and surprised by my honesty.

With so much political correctness to watch out for and people being more self-sensitive than ever before, there is a desperate (and growing) need for truth. Just call things as they are. And be passionate about it. And proud about it. When you do, three amazing things will happen.

One, you will feel great for actually being you and not having to hide behind some crappy wall of fakeness! Two, you will start to get noticed. Three, people will join you and follow you! So many people are desperately searching for leadership – so start leading. Get clear about your own convictions. Then passionately start sharing them with others!

6) **Magic happens when failure is not an option!** I was reminded about it a few days ago when I wrote a Facebook post that stirred quite a conversation. It said, "A lot of people want to talk about achieving success, but few are committed to actually doing what it takes to succeed."

Often my students or clients who tell me how they are going to "try something for 90 days and see how it works" are shocked when I instantly respond with, "I can tell you right now how it's going to work – you will fail!" You see, I believe the very statement of "I will try" sets you up for failure.

When you set out to accomplish anything worthwhile, life will test you. It will get scary at first and very tempting to just turn around and go back where you came from. "Failure is not an option" is not just a cute saying from the "Apollo 13" movie; it's a way of achieving success in every area of life and business by always looking for solutions and never giving up!

Just like I ripped up my return plane ticket and gave myself no option but to succeed, you must take away all alternatives when you are serious about achieving something significant.

7) **Believe in your own magic!** It's sad, but true, that most of us never value ourselves enough. We hugely discount how much

we really have to offer to the world. In fact, this lesson is so important, it deserves its own story.

When I was approached to contribute a chapter to this book, my heart quickly said YES - but my head screamed NO. I instantly loved the idea of "sharing myself" and imparting with you some of the lessons I learned during my journey when "I trusted my heart."

But being a (recovering) perfectionist, I also knew that I would ho and hum for days before I would finally write something I considered worthy of this project that would make a difference in readers' lives. So my mind kicked in with the familiar "tune of gloom" (a.k.a. negative thoughts) of already being too busy with too many projects and that I should just pass.

So I accepted the invitation quickly before my thoughts would overwhelm me with fear and paralyze me into inaction. Then, as I anticipated (see, you always get what you expect) I found myself busy with other projects and procrastinating on writing my chapter until the very, very last minute. (Thank you, Marnie, for being more than patient with me!)

While in my heart I felt my story could inspire others (maybe you) to overcome a difficult situation in life, get started on a "scary" project, or flat out refuse to give in to a current circumstance, the more I thought of writing about my own life, the more scared I felt about actually doing it. "Who would want to read about this?" kept resurfacing in my head over and over again.

Since you are reading this now, I finally did write my story. And here is one final lesson I learned while doing it. (Consider this a bonus lesson.)

We all have a fascinating story that has the power to touch other people's hearts and souls and inspire them to change their lives. But we take this story for granted. We believe it to be too ordinary to share. We feel too timid to reveal it. We feel scared people won't like it, won't find it interesting, or worse, that they will actually ridicule us for imagining we have something worthwhile to say. And thus, so many people (maybe you) go on through their lives with their "song unsung," worrying about other people's opinions instead of living their dreams.

I once heard this joke question, "Why is it best to exercise in the morning?" Answer: "Because it's best to get done with it before your brain wakes up, and you realize what the heck you are doing!" Right now, this very moment, there are things in your life that you are passionate about pursuing. In your heart you hear the calling. But your thoughts make so much noise, you can't make the decision.

Listen to your heart. Take your first step toward your goal right now… and another… and then another. By the time your head "wakes up," you'll be running at full speed toward your goals and the life you want! Get started now!

About Adam Urbanski
As a marketing consultant, Adam Urbanski works with independent service professionals and entrepreneurs, helping them turn their specific knowledge and expertise into profitable revenue centers. He frequently give talks on marketing topics to professional groups and several times a year he teaches an in-depth marketing boot-camp. His website offers more how-to articles and free tips to create a winning marketing action plan at www.TheMarketingMentors.com. Also visit Adam's Info Profit Fast Track at www.InfoProfitFasttrack.com

Conclusion: Miracles Await!

Marnie L. Pehrson

My passion is sharing ideas, truths and the talents of those who have something amazing to offer the world. There's nothing I love more than gathering talented people together in one place so they can share their gifts with a group of people hungry for their messages. That's why I created IdeaMarketers, why I enjoy promoting our experts, and what prompted me to compile this book.

I love connecting people — bringing together talented individuals and letting the synergy loose. Doing it virtually via my website is one thing, but nothing beats gathering a group of gifted people in a live setting. For some time my dream had been to create an event where women could embrace their value, their gifts, and discover how amazing they are. I believe each person on this planet has a purpose — a mission — and that too often we miss it completely, because we never see the treasure lying within ourselves.

My dream was to bring together the right presenters/trainers in the ideal place with the perfect soundtrack. There we'd inspire and assist women who are ready to birth their destinies in a safe, loving environment. That was how the idea for the "Light the World: Birthing Your Destiny" retreat came to be.

Miracle Time Line: The Music Begins

Actually, it all started about six years earlier in 2004, when I was signing *"Lord, Are You Sure?"* at a booksellers' convention booth. At the next table was a young man displaying his piano music CDs. While sitting side-by-side, we introduced ourselves, and I slipped on the earphones to sample his music. I instantly fell in love with Sheldon Pickering's piano music. This unassuming, clean-cut young man endeared me to him every bit as much as his music did. He was the proverbial boy next door with an incredible talent inside him.

In my soul, I heard a voice, "Help this young man." It was a familiar voice — one I'd heard occasionally over the previous decade. When I hear it, I know I'm supposed to assist that person without expecting remuneration. The voice repeated more insistently, "Help this guy."

I started talking to Sheldon about his web presence. He had none. After I got home from the booksellers' convention, I contacted Sheldon and set up a small web site for him within SheLovesGod.com and began selling his CD's to my list. Within a couple years, we lost touch with each other, but I kept listening to Sheldon's two CD's. They became the soundtrack to many of the novels I wrote over the next few years.

Gathering Speakers

In 2008, Lisa Rae Preston signed up as one of our experts at IdeaMarketers.com. By 2009, this jovial, fun-loving, ex-schoolteacher had become a dear friend. Lisa is a personality genius. She knows how people tick and can get to the heart of someone's core passion through a casual conversation. As our friendship progressed, the realization grew clearer that our purposes paralleled. We both help people uncover the treasure within their hearts. I knew a joint project would lie in our future.

Also in 2008, Judy Rankin Hansen purchased my *"You're Here for a Reason: Discover & Live Your Purpose"* book. I was running a special offer where anyone who bought the book would receive a 30-minute consult with me. It took a few months before our schedules connected, but what started as a 30-minute consult turned into a 3-hour conversation. I instantly knew this woman had an amazing gift. She is a born energy-intuitive with the uncanny ability to see energy and potential in everyone and everything around her. The idea of helping her take such an ethereal gift and "package" it for the benefit of the world intrigued me. Once again, I heard that voice, "Help this lady."

In October of 2009, my friend Leslie Householder had a last-minute opening at her writer retreat in Flagstaff, Arizona. She called me on Friday afternoon before the retreat started on Monday and suggested I take the opening. At the time, I wasn't one to pick up and fly somewhere on a moment's notice. But I felt I should go. I bought my ticket immediately, flew out on Sunday and joined Leslie for her retreat.

There, I met 4 other women who were writing books about the dramatic circumstances of their lives and what they'd learned from them. I watched these ladies struggle to be authentic, transparent and share their experiences in a vulnerable way. It was a difficult time for them as they relived the past and wrestled to put it down on paper in a way that wasn't "poor me" but conveyed their stories in inspirational ways.

As I watched them struggle, I knew my friend Judy Hansen could help. Using her gifts of reading energy and potential, she's amazing at helping people find clarity about their purpose via a visual journey — a guided meditation or what Judy calls an "enscript." I suggested to Leslie that I invite Judy down to see if she could help the women with their projects. Leslie agreed, and Judy hopped in a car that very afternoon and arrived by evening. Sure enough, she proved to be a valuable resource to these ladies — especially two of them who would later end up attending the Light the World Retreat.

Watching the Pieces Fit Together

It was at Leslie's retreat that Judy and I got the idea for doing our own event to help women birth their destinies. We went back to our homes and began brainstorming this idea. As I mentioned it to Lisa Rae Preston, I felt very strongly that she should be a part of this event. I recommended her to Judy, and the three of us agreed to meet in Salt Lake City in December of 2009, to talk about the planning.

Lisa and Judy immediately hit it off, and we spent a week, praying, meditating, and discussing the possibility of bringing women together and helping them discover their God-given missions and live them with courage, vision and fearlessness. We found the perfect location, set the date and started discussing our team.

Ironically, Sheldon Pickering (the pianist) had recently contacted me out of the blue on Facebook and wanted to make more of his music available to people online. So as we put together our ideal team, I knew Sheldon had to be a part of Light the World, too.

In one of my earlier visits to Judy's house, she'd let me listen to some of her daughter's violin music. Masterful, passionate, and enlivening!

Again, I felt strongly that this talented musician (Jamie Bartschi) should be a part of the retreat. Though I'd never even met her, I knew she would fit. Both her music and her insights from life would grace our gathering perfectly.

We scheduled the event for April 2010 in Zion National Park, a place I'd come to love from recent visits. It has an incredible energy and makes you feel like if God can create something so majestic in nature, He could easily create something magical in your life.

So Close, and Yet So Far!

We had the place, the presenters, and the music. Now all we needed were the participants. Over the next four months we marketed the event. It was slow-going, and we wondered if we'd sign up enough people to break even. Additionally, we experienced a series of bizarre twists and turns that would have made anyone in their right mind throw in the towel. One of my main sites was continually hacked by foreigners — absorbing most of my time and attention. There were more relationship issues, family dramas, and business challenges amongst us than we would have experienced in several years — all crammed into a 4-month period.

We pressed on. At those times when I felt like cancelling the event, one thing kept me going. I knew from experience that you either push through your trials or you're doomed to circle back around to them. I had no desire to go through this mess again, so I pushed on through.

Victory! The Beauty Unfolds...

Finally, the time for the event came, and we had 15 beautiful participants there, ready and willing to birth their destinies. Each one had been uniquely prepared. I could not have asked for a more amazing group of women.

I remember standing at the back of the room watching them eat lunch. I realized that this event had been in the making since I first sat down next to Sheldon Pickering seven years earlier. Had I ignored those impressions to "Help this person," I never would have collected the people who would make my heart's dream come true.

I've set and achieved many goals in my life. Most of the time I feel a let-down afterward as if to say, "That was it? I made that big of a deal out of that?" The Light the World event is the one thing in my life I never felt that way about. It was more incredible, more amazing than anything I ever imagined. It's the gift that keeps on giving. I just think about it and feel better. I keep in touch with the women, and they remain an important part of my life.

I recorded all the music from the event and listen to it often. Jamie with her violin and Sheldon with his piano and synthesizer made a perfect pair. There was one piece of music called "Mercy's Arms" that I wanted performed on the third day, but Jamie couldn't find the music for it. Neither she nor Sheldon were familiar with the piece. Then, out of the blue on the third evening, one of the women asked if she could sing and play a song. I agreed that she could - not knowing what song she intended to play.

Can you imagine my surprise as she sat down and played the exact song I had on my wish list for that night? It was beautiful, heart-felt perfection. Tears of wonderment filled my eyes as I realized heaven took care of my finest details — down to a song I wanted sung on a particular evening!

When you have a dream that involves helping other people, don't hold anything back. Make your wish list. There was a time I felt God telling me, "What do you want, Marnie? Make a list of your perfect team, your perfect place, your ideal participants. Whatever you want, I want to give it to you."

He did! And some! When you are living your purpose and being of service to your fellow-beings, you are entitled to all the abundance you need to make your dream happen. Doubt not. Fear not. Miracles await!

30 Lessons I Learned from Going for My Dream

While Lisa, Judy and I were planning the Light the World event together, we caught the vision of something incredible, something beautiful. We saw what God can do with righteous women who love Him and who serve in their own unique ways, exactly where they stand. We left Southern Utah excited, hopeful and full of faith.

Little did we know that when we returned to put in motion what we'd seen in vision, we'd be hit with a series of challenges that would make us question our vision and test our friendships, families, and faith.

What helped me endure the obstacles was seeing them in a different way. Rather than assuming we were doing something incredible and now had targets on our backs for Satan's archery practice, I decided to look at them as blessings. What if each trial we endured was there to teach us something valuable that we needed to know? What if the challenges would shape us into the people we needed to be to effectively help these women come April 2010?

As I began looking at my challenges in this way, I found the gems within them. Once the spiritual lesson was learned, the trial resolved itself and moved onto the next one.

I began itemizing the challenges – not dwelling on the details – but listing the lessons learned from them. As I did so, I realized that I'd gained a lifetime of knowledge in a three-month period. It would take most people years to learn these kinds of lessons in a practical, experiential way.

Here are a few of them I learned (or re-learned):

1. Get to the root of problems. You could spend weeks trying to treat the symptoms whereas fixing the root could take minutes.

2. When faced with a daunting challenge, avoid going straight into workaholic, production mode. Rather, step back and ask God for His perspective. Ask Him to help you get to the root.

3. Avoid the quick "please help me with this" kind of prayers. Have a real conversation with God about your challenge and ask for something specific you should do. Many times the solutions to monumental challenges are incredibly simple. And God knows what they are! But if you don't take the time to consult with Him, it's harder for Him to tell you.

4. Sometimes sickness can be a blessing to help you step back and look at things differently.

5. Communicate specifically. Don't assume other people understand what you're thinking or even trying to say.

6. Just because you have a hobby you love doesn't mean you should turn it into a business.

7. When you build a life around something that ends up making you miserable, don't shift the blame to the people who helped you along the way.

8. Never abdicate your responsibility to receive your own answers. Other people can be wise and spiritual and give excellent advice. But bottom line, you need to get your own answers. You will be tested later, and if you haven't gotten your own confirmation, doubt will be a monster that plagues you.

9. Everyone's human. Looking for the good in others is a wonderful thing, but don't put people on pedestals. No one is always following the Spirit. No one is always making the best choices. We're all human. It's unfair to expect perfection in others.

10. Some people are never going to apologize. Forgive them anyway.

11. Forgiveness has the power to erase the pain, the hurt and leave the lesson. God really can diminish the memory of a recent offense so that it loses its sting.

12. Never stick your head in the sand and hope problems will resolve themselves. Turn and face challenges head on, get to the root and get help quickly.

13. Be careful to never make other people feel that your path should be their path. Let them know they need to ask, seek, and know what's right for them.

14. What everyone else thinks is the "right" thing for you to be or do could be the worst thing for you.

15. Gratitude is a hallmark of character.

16. A sign of spiritual maturity is that we celebrate, acknowledge and love each other for our unique gifts and perspectives. Celebrating and acknowledging you and what you've done in my life doesn't diminish me in any way.

17. The desires of our hearts govern our outcomes, thus the importance of getting down to your core values, core passions and purpose. Be careful what you wish for! It might show up on your doorstep.

18. Working harder can be a curse. When you think you have to fix everything yourself by working harder, you get in workhorse blinder mode and miss the obvious, little things that could simply and elegantly make things flow.

19. Just because people are around you and see your example of a principle doesn't mean they will understand or embrace that principle. They must desire to learn and be asking the right questions.

20. Putting on a façade takes a lot of energy and stress. Being authentic and willing to let people know you are human is a more energy-efficient and effective way to live. You experience more joy, more peace, and more grace.

21. In the pursuit of your dream, some people will interpret the hard things you endure as evidence you shouldn't be doing what you are doing. Just because you face hardships doesn't mean God is

telling you you're off track. Only you can know your integrity (remember Job).

22. The vision we receive of the future rarely happens overnight.

23. When we ask God for a vision, He tends to show us only as far ahead as we can safely see. What you desire may not be delivered on the time table you think or want.

24. Never give up. Giving up means you'll have to start over.

25. Use your brain and be practical, even in the face of a big vision.

26. Trust God's time table even when it looks like His timing is making your life difficult.

27. Stay focused on the positive.

28. Shift out of fear the moment it rears its ugly head.

29. Find ways to maintain the vision, even when it looks impossible.

30. One of the greatest blessings you can have is friends who believe in and work alongside you in your vision. Thank God for them every single day! They may be the greatest miracles of all.

Through it all, I've come to remember that God never wastes the pain. The greatest treasures come from our trials.

I encourage you, wherever you are, whatever dreams are held close in your own heart – submit them to the power of God so He can fuel them for birthing. Your dreams were given, not just to inspire you on a day of drudgery, but to bring into glorious reality!

Clarify your purpose, hold to your dream, never give up, and above all...trust your heart!

Listen to exclusive interviews with the experts featured in this book at www.TrustYourHeartSeries.com

Resources Available to Help You Transform Your Ideas to Income:

FREE *Ideas to Income Magazine*
http://www.TheIdeaMag.com

Promote Your Articles, Press Releases, Information Products, Audios, Videos and Expertise for free at
http://www.IdeaMarketers.com

Raise Your Abundance Quotient
http://www.AbundanceQuotient.com

Monetize Your Gifts
http://www.MonetizeYourGifts.com

Find More Books & Resources by Marnie Pehrson at
http://www.MarniePehrson.com

CPSIA information can be obtained at www.ICGtesting.com
Printed in the USA
LVOW130828260512

283412LV00006B/107/P